D1174849

Prayer
Book
Rubrics
EXPANDED

Byron D. Stuhlman

THE CHURCH HYMNAL CORPORATION, NEW YORK

The extensive quotation in the Introduction from J.J. von Allmen, *Worship: Its Theology and Practice,* is printed by permission of the publishers, Lutterworth Press, London.

Rubrics are cited from the following sources:

The Book of Common Prayer, Church Pension Fund, New York, 1979.

Lesser Feasts and Fasts, copyright 1980, Church Pension Fund, New York.

The Book of Occasional Services, copyright 1979, Church Pension Fund, New York.

The quotation in the Introduction from Marion J. Hatchett, *Sanctifying Life, Time, and Space,* is printed by permission of the publishers, Seabury Press, Harper and Row.

The Church Hymnal Corporation
800 Second Avenue
New York, NY 10017

10   9   8   7   6   5   4   3   2   1

Table of Contents

Acknowledgements

I am grateful to many who have contributed to my love and knowledge for the liturgy of the Church, and especially to the Rev. H. Boone Porter, who taught me liturgics at General Seminary; the Rev. Richard Corney, who taught me to celebrate the Eucharist; to the Rt. Rev. Warren Hutchins, the Rt. Rev. Morgan Porteus, and the Rt. Rev. Arthur Walmsley, Bishops of Connecticut, under whom I served as chair of the diocesan Liturgical Commission; to Raymond Glover, who is in large part responsible for my knowledge of the church's musical tradition; and to the people of God in Christ Church Cathedral, Hartford, Connecticut, St. Mark's Church, Bridgewater, Connecticut, and the Church of St. Thomas of Canterbury, Sherman, Connecticut, to whom I have ministered in worship as a presbyter of the Church.

I am also grateful to those who read this manuscript and offered suggestions: the Rev. Carl Daw, the Rev. Henry Breul, the Rev. Canon Charles Guilbert, the Rev. Louis Weil, and the Rev. Thomas Talley.

Finally, I extend my thanks to Frank Hemlin and the Church Hymnal Corporation, at whose initiative this book was written, and to Gregory Eaton, who saw the manuscript through to publication.

Byron David Stuhlman
Maundy Thursday, 1987

Preface

The evolution of liturgical worship encompassses more than merely changes in the texts of authorized rites. The manner in which those rites are celebrated, the pastoral priorities which are manifested in a particular liturgical style, complement the texts as they give expression to the Church's faith.

For Anglicans, this complementary dimension has been associated with the rubrics of each rite. For some clergy, the rubrics have been thought to indicate everything that was needed for the proper celebration of a rite. Yet in practice this was never the case. The rubrics of *The Book of Common Prayer* supplied the ritual framework—one might say the ritual minimum—of each liturgical action, but the rites were always celebrated in a particular building under specific conditions which inevitably shaped the way the rubrics were interpreted. Further, a rite was always celebrated from within a specific tradition and ethos which determined, often at an unconscious level, the expectations of both clergy and laity of the style, whether simple or elaborate, in which the celebrations would take place.

It is to this further dimension, this aspect which rubrics are never able to encompass, that Byron Stuhlman's *Prayer Book Rubrics Expanded* is addressed. It is a book which has been needed ever since *The Book of Common Prayer* 1979 demonstrated a transformed understanding of the role of rubrics. In themselves, the rubrics are clearly intended as minimalist indications of the shape of a particular rite, whereas their flexibility indicates that they cannot address every possible variation in the pastoral context. Further, the systematic inclusion of material Concerning the Service prior to each rite, and Additional Directions at its conclusion, offers a kind of theological/pastoral framework in which the unfolding of each celebration is to be realized. The way this material is presented in *The Book of Common Prayer* 1979 is a clear sign that the Church has moved beyond the type of rubrical fundamentalism which sees a rite as a kind of liturgical drill.

In this perspective, *The Book of Common Prayer* is a sign of a much wider shift in approach in all the liturgical churches to the nature of liturgical celebrations. Whereas the common ground of the authorized texts and the general rubrical framework manifests one of the fundamental expressions of our unity within the Anglican tradition, it is a principle of the American Prayer Book that this shared tradition must be interpreted and implemented afresh within the ecclesial and pastoral realities of the local church. As a special responsibility of the ordained clergy, liturgical leadership in this regard requires more than the repetition of a fixed pattern and routine. It demands an ability to reflect both theologically and pastorally from within a given Christian community on the ways in which the Prayer Book tradition can become the living prayer of the local community in its particularity.

Many of our clergy were not prepared by their seminary education to see their liturgical responsibility in these terms. Only in very recent years has liturgical formation begun to address this new approach which sees liturgical rites as rooted in the reality of a specific community's life. *Prayer Book Rubrics Expanded* is not merely another "how to do it" manual for the clergy. It effectively points us to the deeper level of the relation of liturgical rites to the pastoral reality of the Church's life, in which the assembled community finds its self-realization as the people of God.

Louis Weil
Nashotah House, 1987

"It is a most invaluable part of the blessed 'liberty with which Christ has made us free,' that in his worship different forms and usages may without offense be allowed, provided that the substance of the Faith be kept entire...."

—THE BOOK OF COMMON PRAYER
Preface (1789)

Introduction

Historically, ceremonial instruction for Anglican worship has taken two forms. The first form is the directions (sometimes called rubrics, because they have often been printed in red) contained in the Book of Common Prayer. The second form is ceremonial guidelines which expand upon the rubrics. In the present edition of *The Book of Common Prayer*, the rubrics are found in four places:

1. "Concerning the Service of the Church" and "The Calendar of the Church Year" on pages 15–18 provide general directions for the conduct of all services in the book.

2. Many services in the book and some sections of other material are preceded by general directions for their use, entitled "Concerning..."

3. The text of services itself contains directions (usually in italics) necessary for following the service.

4. Many services are followed by "Additional Directions" about specific details of the service which are not necessary for following the service and which would unnecessarily clutter the text if printed in the body of the service.

Similar directions are given in *The Book of Occasional Services* and the book of *Lesser Feasts and Fasts,* which are officially authorized supplements to *The Book of Common Prayer.* Directions for the use of music in worship are provided in *The Hymnal, Gradual Psalms, Music for Ministers and Congregations,* and *The Altar Book.*

Rubrical directions in the Prayer Book are generally of three kinds.

1. *Normative rubrics* in the present book are generally in the present indicative: "is, reads, stand, sit, kneel." Others use words or phrases such as "shall, is directed, is required" or a form of "be" with the infinitive.

2. *Rubrics which recommend* a certain action generally use such words or phrases as "it is customary; it is fitting; it is desirable; it is recommended; where practicable; where appropriate."

3. *Permissive rubrics* are usually indicated by the word "may." They indicate options without making a requirement or recommendation.

The usual interpretation of the Prayer Book has been that only those texts may be used which are explicitly indicated, but that ceremonial actions and gestures are permissible unless explicitly forbidden. Canon Charles Guilbert, present custodian of the Standard Book of Common Prayer, describes the rubrics of the Prayer Book as "descriptive, not prescriptive." This has resulted in a broad spectrum of ways in which an identical service is conducted in different congregations and circumstances.

The official and binding directions of *The Book of Common Prayer* thus do not prescribe a single "correct" way of conducting a service. They set forth which service is appropriate for a specific situation, what roles are proper to lay persons and to the various orders of ordained ministers who participate, what is required in terms of liturgical space and equipment, and what the essential words and actions are. Beyond this, they allow a large measure of flexibility.

The liturgy of the classical Roman Rite of the seventh century has been described as severe, sober, restrained, conservative, and characterized by a direct simplicity. Ceremonial actions were practical in nature. Texts were tightly constructed and brief and usually followed the rules of rhetorical cursus. Later, as it was used elsewhere, this rite was adapted to different tastes. In its later form, it was characterized by a love of color, ceremony, and ornamentation, and lost much of its directness, simplicity, brevity, and restraint. Anglican liturgy in its pristine form had the same traits as the classical Roman Rite. In great churches, however, and on great occasions, it took on the love of color, ceremony, and ornamentation of the later Roman Rite. It is this more ceremonial form of worship which most people think of when they think of Anglican worship. The true genius of the Anglican Rite, like that of the Roman Rite, however, is found in its pristine form. Episcopalians would do well to be wary of that ceremoniousness which obscures the evangelical simplicity of their worship and is in fact more cultural than religious in its appeal.

Because of the flexibility of the official and binding rubrical directions of the Prayer Book itself, Anglicans have customarily used a second form of ceremonial instruction—ceremonial guides which are unofficial and non-binding. Manuals for leaders in worship (clergy, lay readers, acolytes, musicians) and devotional guides for the congregation provide supplemental directions or rubrics.

These books reflect the whole spectrum of the Anglican theology and liturgical tradition. The labels attached to parts of this spectrum are notoriously imprecise, but it is well to note them at least in general terms. When the emphasis is on the style of ceremonial, the terms are generally "high-church," "broad-church," and "low-church." When the emphasis is on the theological tradition to which the ceremonial gives expression, the terms are generally "catholic," "latitudinarian," and "evangelical."

The catholic or high-church end of the spectrum tends to give ceremonial expression to the continuity of Anglican worship with catholic tradition. The evangelical or low-church end of the spectrum tends to give ceremonial expression to the ties of Anglican worship with continental reformed churches. Latitudinarian or broad church ceremonial has generally sought a style which is acceptable to the average Anglican. At times, the ends of the spectrum seem to define Anglican theology and Anglican worship primarily in terms of another tradition, and the center of the spectrum seems more like a compromise than a synthesis. While catholic and evangelical preferences are noted from time to time in this book, on the whole the labels foster a partisan spirit and are best avoided.

Thoughtful Anglicans down through the ages have believed that besides these traditions there is a genuinely *Anglican* tradition for which no further label is appropriate—a tradition which embodies a distinctively Anglican theology. Marion Hatchett, in *Sanctifying Life, Time, and Space* (page 114), sets out four principles for Anglican worship drawn for the writings of Archbishop Cranmer in 1549: it is

(1) *"grounded upon the holy Scriptures"*; (2) *"agreeable to the order of the primitive church"*; (3) *unifying to the realm; and* (4) *"edifying"* to the people.

While we would probably prefer that worship be "unifying to the Church" rather than to the "realm" and might also add "appropriate to the pastoral situation," Cranmer's principles have stood the test of time. In fact, they underlie the work of the liturgical movement of the past century and so have ecumenical relevance as well. At the present moment the best Christian liturgy reflects a remarkable theological and liturgical convergence, and within the Episcopal Church there is a similar convergence which renders the earlier "schools of churchmanship" largely dated.

It is this emerging spirit of convergence in the Christian Church as a whole and within the Episcopal Church in particular which underlies the expanded or supplemental rubrics of this book. The book presupposes a certain aesthetic of worship which the author believes to be truly catholic and truly evangelical. The Second Vatican Council set as its standard a "noble simplicity" of liturgical expression. But I believe that it is the Swiss Reformed liturgist J.J. von Allmen who puts it best (*Worship: Its Theology and Practice*, pages 102–104 *passim*):

...The fact remains that simplicity is an important condition of true worship. It is not to be confused with baldness, negligence of forms or a docetic impatience with regard to forms. It is rather a matter of concentration, a determination to base worship on the central issues. We mighty also say that it reflects a desire to show that the cult in fact sums up the work of Him in whom God has summed up all things: whence come a sense of order, a pruning of all that savours of the baroque. It also produces a great vigilance as regards symbols. Simplicity... is in the first instance the opposite not of complexity, but of diffuseness... It is a respect for the structure controlling the relation between the various parts of the cult, in an arrangement which shows that the cult progresses toward its culminating point, and that, having reached it, it is strengthened by it for the purpose of afterwards witnessing in the world....

...To beautify the cult, we must not enrich it but purify it. True beauty is a school of purgation, it resists everything that is self-centered: it is grace and harmony, severe toward the flourishes and excrescences of an aesthetic self-centeredness. That is why respect for beauty will not lead us to embellish the cult—as one bedecks an old lady with make-up—but it will try to show that the cult cannot fail to be beautiful if it is true...

Liturgical beauty is a protest, not only against all aesthetic self-centeredness, but also against negligence, coarseness, casualness, and in general against vulgar familiarity. The very fact that the cult is an encounter between the Lord and the Church implies an ennobling of this encounter and a glorification of the Lord who deigns to be present.

I wish to make clear my meaning in saying that beauty is a condition of true worship: I mean that worship, if conducted with faith, hope and love, engenders beauty, and supplies a basis of radical criticism of self-centered aestheticism and vulgarity. The cult can be very poor without ceasing to be beautiful, and it will probably cease to be beautiful if it aspires to become rich. But "poor" does not mean shabby or sad or cheap. "Poor" means to be without, not form or symbols, but without pretence or self-centeredness.

CHAPTER I

Preliminary Essentials

Before we turn our attention to directions and suggestions for particular services, there are certain preliminary matters that we must consider: **(1)** the pattern of worship presupposed by *The Book of Common Prayer* and its theological basis; **(2)** the participants in worship and their function and vesture; **(3)** the setting of worship— "the house of the church"; **(4)** ceremonial action; **(5)** the language of the liturgy; and **(6)** the use of music.

The Pattern of Christian Worship

The first matter to be considered is one that frequently escapes our attention altogether. *The Book of Common Prayer* is not a miscellaneous collection of services; it provides a pattern for our worship that sets forth the appropriate service for each situation. If we do not understand this, our use of the Prayer Book will easily get off course.

The first rubric of *The Book of Common Prayer* 1979 states:

The Holy Eucharist, the principal act of Christian worship on the Lord's Day and other major feasts, and Daily Morning and Evening Prayer, as set forth in this Book, are the regular services appointed for public worship in this Church.

This rubric makes explicit what was implicit in all prior editions of *The Book of Common Prayer*: that the Prayer Book prescribes a pattern of services for parochial worship—*daily* Morning and Evening Prayer and the Holy Eucharist *on Sundays and other major feasts for which propers are provided.* A "regular" service in this sense is one which is *regulated* by the calendar of the church year and the lectionaries of the Prayer Book.

Daily Morning and Evening Prayer is rooted in the tradition of the Church and ultimately in its heritage from the Jewish synagogue. These services form the first major section of service material in the Prayer Book, *The Daily Office.* Also included in this section are two other parts of the Office which may be used as occasion requires—An Order of Service for Noonday and An Order for Compline, as well as a festive form of Evening Prayer—An Order of Worship for the Evening, and informal Daily Devotions for Individuals and Families. The Great Litany, prescribed by earlier Prayer Books for use after Morning Prayer on certain days, follows.

The occasions for which the celebration of the Eucharist are prescribed are theologically grounded. Sundays, "the first day of the week," when Christ "overcame death and the grave, and by his glorious resurrection opened to us the way of everlasting life" (Preface 2 of the Lord's Day, pages 345 and 377), are for that reason "feasts of our Lord Jesus Christ." They and other feasts of Christ are appropriately observed by the celebration of the Eucharist in which the "Risen Lord" is "known to us in the breaking of the Bread" (Eucharistic Prayer C, page 372). The feasts of the saints are observed in the same way because (*Lesser Feasts and Fasts,* page 56)

> ...the triumphs of the saints are a continuation and manifestation of the Paschal victory of Christ...

For the major feasts of the Calendar, the celebration of the Eucharist is prescribed; other feasts listed on the calendar are days of optional commemoration, along with the weekdays of Lent and Easter. Propers for these optional commemorations are found in the book of *Lesser Feasts and Fasts*. The Eucharist is not appropriate on Good Friday and Holy Saturday, days which commemorate Christ's death and burial.

The propers in the Prayer Book for Various Occasions are not commemorations; they are provided for what have been known in the West as "votive celebrations," celebrations related to a theme or intention rather than to the calendar. They may not replace the major feasts of the calendar, but may be used at other times. A daily celebration of the Eucharist (except on Good Friday and Holy Saturday) is neither required nor forbidden. The daily celebration of the Eucharist does tend to blur the distinction between feasts and other days, however, and overshadow the office as the proper form of daily worship.

The Collects for the Church Year, the section of the Prayer Book following the Great Litany, are provided for use with the regular services—that is, the Daily Office and the Holy Eucharist. Rubrics in this section regulate the use of the various propers.

The Proper Liturgies and Holy Baptism, the sections printed before the Holy Eucharist in the Prayer Book, may also be understood as "regular services"—that is, as services regulated by the calendar. The Proper Liturgies are special forms of the Proclamation of the Word of God used in Lent and Holy Week and at the Great Vigil of Easter. *The Book of Occasional Services* also provides proper liturgies. These include baptismal vigils for the Baptism of Christ and All Saints' Day or Sunday, other special forms of the Ministry of the Word on other days; seasonal material for the Office (lucernaria, or lamplighting responsories), the Eucharist (confractoria, or fraction anthems), and blessings; materials for the catechumenate for use in Lent or Advent; and seasonal services which are, properly speaking, paraliturgical. All of the material from this book is for *optional and supplementary use.*

Holy Baptism, formerly considered an occasional office, is now understood as the proper service for the baptismal feasts—Easter, Pentecost, the Baptism of Christ, and All Saints' Day or Sunday—and for the Bishop's visitation. The baptismal Eucharist is *the proper liturgy for these feasts*; in the absence of candidates for Baptism on these days, the Renewal of Baptismal Vows should replace the Creed at the Eucharist (rubric, pages 312; form, pages 292–294). A special bidding is provided for the Easter renewal of vows and one might be composed for the other days, relating the theology of Baptism to the theology of these feasts. A procession to the font would also be appropriate on these days, with a blessing of the water using the form provided on pages 570–571 and perhaps an aspersion of the congregation. The rubric on page 298 tells us that the baptismal Eucharist is *an appropriate liturgy* for any Sunday or feast. Baptism should not be administered at other times except in an emergency.

As distinct from these *regular* services, the Pastoral Offices and Episcopal Services in the Prayer Book and similar materials in *The Book of Occasional Services* are *occasional* services—that is, their use is determined by occasions in the lives of individuals and congregations rather than by the calendar. Note the second and third rubrics on page 13 of the Prayer Book:

> *In addition to these services [the regular services] and the other rites contained in this book, other forms set forth by authority within this Church may also be used. Also, subject to the direction of the bishop, special devotions taken from this Book, or from Holy Scripture, may be used when the needs of the congregation require.*

> *For special days of fasting or thanksgiving, appointed by civil or Church authority, and for other special occasions for which no service or prayer has been provided in this Book, the bishop may set forth such forms as are fitting to the occasion.*

These rubrics cover:

1. Pastoral Offices and Episcopal Services ("other rites contained in this Book");

2. Services in *The Book of Occasional Services* ("other forms set forth by authority");

3. "Special devotions" to meet the particular needs of a congregation, subject to the bishop's direction;

4. Forms for special days of fasting or thanksgiving set forth by the bishop.

It is important to be attentive to this pattern and its rhythms, in order that Christian worship reflect and embody the proportion and balance of Christian theology. Today, the Prayer Book pattern is recognized as true to the best Catholic and Evangelical tradition; its observance should not become a matter of controversy, as it was often in the past.

The Participants in Worship and their Function and Vesture

Recent liturgical theology has described worship as the epiphany of the Church—the situation in which the true character of the Church is revealed. Consequently, the functions of the members of the Church in the life of the Church are revealed by their functions as participants in the Church's worship. All Christians by virtue of their baptism share in the royal priesthood of Christ and in Christ's ministry of reconciliation. This is made explicit in *The Book of Common Prayer* 1979 by the references to this royal priesthood in the forms for the consecration of chrism and for the welcoming of the newly baptized on pages 307 and 308 and by the answer to the question, "Who are the ministers of the Church?", on page 855 in the Catechism.

The Episcopal Church's present understanding of ministry is stated most clearly in the Preface to the Ordination Rites on page 510 and in the section in the Catechism entitled "The Ministry" on pages 855 and 856. On the whole, it represents a recovery of a biblical and patristic theology of ministry which was partly displaced in the Middle Ages. Its key insight is the doctrine of the royal priesthood and of the ministry of reconciliation which is conferred by baptism. Unfortunately, the wording of the catechism gives the impression that lay persons constitute an order of ministry equivalent to the three orders of ordained ministers. Properly speaking, both the ordained and those not ordained share a common ministry by virtue of their baptism; besides this common ministry each order of the ordained has special functions within the ministry of the Church. The answer to the first question in this section of the catechism might better be phrased, "All Christians are ministers of the Church by virtue of their baptism," and the second question might better be worded, "What is the ministry which we share by virtue of our baptism?". Apart from the catechism, the Prayer Book ordinarily reverts to the older usage and means "ordained minister" when it says "minister."

Canon Charles Guilbert, commenting on the usage of the word minister in the rubrics of the 1979 Book writes (letter to the author dated May 25, 1987):

> *The Standing Liturgical Commission strove to clarify the older ambiguous usage of "minister" by the use of "celebrant," "officiant," or the specific order of ordained ministry when such distinction is intended. The exceptions are very few:* **(1)** *some of the rubrics of the Rite One Eucharist, where close adherence to the 1928 rite was aimed at;* **(2)** *"Minister of the Congregation" to denote the person, clerical or lay, to whom the notice of illness or death is to be made;* **(3)** *ministers of other denominations who might be participating in Prayer-Book rites; and* **(4)** *additional members of the altar team, called "other ministers," which would include both lay and clerical members."*

There is a similar ambiguity in regard to the use of the word "priest." The word itself is ambiguous in English, being derived from the Latin for presbyter but usually carrying the meaning of the Latin word for priest (sacerdos). The liturgical texts of Baptism speak of the priesthood of the baptized. The rubrics of the book, however, use the word to refer to ordained priests. Properly speaking the orders of the ordained ministry are bishops, presbyters, and deacons. These are separate and distinct orders of ministry, each with its specific functions. First bishops, and then presbyters, came to be called priests. In the Middle Ages, the orders of ministry came to be understood not as functions within the ministry of the Church, but as participation, in varying degrees, in the priesthood of Christ. In other words, bishops, presbyters, and deacons were understood as chief priests,

priests, and apprentice priests. As one scholar notes, an omnivorous presbyterate devoured the other orders of ordained ministry.

The present Prayer Book operates generally with the patristic idea of three separate and distinct orders of ministry rather than with a hierarchical ladder where one advances from diaconate to priesthood and a few advance further to the episcopate. It continues to use "priest" for "presbyter," however, probably partly out of a desire to maintain that the presbyterate is a priestly ministry. At other times, as in the rite for Communion under Special Circumstances and that for the Reconciliation of a Penitent, "priest" is to be understood as "bishop or presbyter." Although the usage of the rubrics is somewhat inconsistent and ambiguous, the context usually makes the meaning clear.

What are the functions of these orders of ministry? They are set forth in the Preface to the Ordination Rites, page 510. Bishops "carry on the work of leading, supervising, and uniting the Church." Presbyters, as associates of the bishops, "take part in the governance of the Church, in carrying out its missionary and pastoral work, and in the preaching of the Word of God and administering his holy Sacraments." Deacons "assist bishops and priests [= presbyters] in this work."

These general functions are revealed in the way each order functions in worship. The functions are set out in general terms in the directions on page 14 of the Prayer Book "Concerning the Service of the Church":

> In all services, the entire Christian assembly participates in such a way that the members of each order within the Church, lay persons, bishops, priests [= presbyters] and deacons fulfill the functions proper to their respective orders, as set forth in the rubrical directions for each service.
>
> The leader of worship in a Christian assembly is normally a bishop or priest [= presbyter]. Deacons by virtue of their order do not exercise a presiding function; but, like lay persons, may officiate at the Liturgy of the Word, whether in the form provided in the Daily Offices, or (when a bishop or priest [= presbyter] is not present) in the form appointed at the Eucharist. Under exceptional circumstances, when the services of a priest [= presbyter] cannot be obtained, the bishop may, at discretion,

authorize a deacon to preside at other rites also, subject to the limitations described in the directions for each service.

The initial directions concerning each service give more specifics, as do the rubrics in the text of services and the additional directions printed after them. In particular we see in this Prayer Book much more careful attention to the appropriate functions of deacons and lay persons, whose parts in the service should not be usurped by bishops and presbyters.

For most of the Church's history, Christians have considered it appropriate to clothe those with special functions in public worship with particular vesture, both for seemliness and to indicate their office and function. This is true today, although there is presently a certain freedom to omit vestments on occasions of informal worship. In the Church of England, the vesture of ministers has been regulated by rubric and canon. The Episcopal Church for most of its history in this country has not officially regulated the vesture of its ministers at all. The only explicit requirements of *The Book of Common Prayer* 1979 are that candidates for ordination be presented in an alb or surplice (for the diaconate and presbyterate) or in an alb or rochet (for the episcopate).

We will treat the vesture of ministers by noting first the vestments and insignia of office in common use, then looking at the usage through history (by regulation or custom) in the Church of England, and finally by making suggestions for the Episcopal Church today.

Vestments in Use:

Basic Vestments. The *cassock* is properly speaking not a vestment at all, but the street dress of clerics. Since it is not in fact generally worn this way today, it may be (and often is) omitted, except with the surplice and the older forms of the rochet. The basic Christian vestment is the *alb,* a full-length white tunic with narrow sleeves. It was in origin the basic undergarment of the Roman empire. Since Christians were clothed in a clean white tunic when they came forth from the baptismal washing, this came to be considered the appropriate garb of the baptized, symbolic of the purity bestowed in baptism. It is an appropriate garment for any person with a particular function in public worship. Traditionally it has been girded with a *cincture* and worn with either a neckpiece (*amice*) or a hood. Contemporary forms of this garment have a high collar or hood in place of the amice and may be worn girded or ungirded. These contemporary forms, worn without cassock, often are cut like a double-breasted cassock and are consequently easier to put on than the traditional form of the garment. The most common variant is often known as the "cassock-alb" for this reason.

Two other variants of the alb have developed over the centuries. The *surplice* is in origin an alb of ample proportions and full sleeves, large enough to be worn over a fur-lined cassock. In the Middle Ages it came to be worn by all those with functions in public worship who were not vested as eucharistic ministers. Originally (and at the time of the Reformation in England) ankle-length, it tended to shrink to a waist-length vestment over the centuries. This latter form is not terribly attractive, and current taste favors a form no shorter than below the knees. Since it requires a cassock underneath, there has been a trend in recent years to replace the surplice with the alb for all uses.

The *rochet* is a fuller form of the alb, either with or without sleeves, worn ungirded over the cassock. Today it is commonly worn by bishops. Until recently the form worn by them had full sleeves gathered at the wrist with bands. In more modern forms it is indistinguishable from the alb. With the *chimere* (a sleeveless black or scarlet gown), an academic hood, and a black *scarf,* it constituted parliamentary robes for English bishops and eventually was worn by them when they did not use eucharistic vestments or the cope.

Overvestments. Over the alb, clergy with particular functions at the Eucharist traditionally wear another set of vestments. The *chasuble,* in its ancient and contemporary form a kind of poncho, was ordinary street wear for citizens of the Roman empire, and as such was used by clergy at worship. Later it was restricted to the bishop or presbyter who presided at the Eucharist and conformed to the liturgical color of the celebration. In the last century broad church Anglicans sometimes adopted the custom of wearing a white linen chasuble for all eucharists, and all-purpose chasubles are not uncommon today. The vestment itself is symbolic of presidency at the Eucharist; the elaborate ornamentation customary in the Middle Ages has fallen out of favor at the present time, and only bands or orphreys are generally used to ornament the chasuble today.

The *dalmatic* and *tunicle* are short tunics with wide sleeves worn over the alb. The dalmatic was in origin a vestment of honor, worn first by the bishop and later by his deacons in public worship. The tunicle was worn by the subdeacon at the Eucharist and was indistinguishable from the dalmatic except for different treatment of the orphreys. The Prayer Book of 1549 makes no distinction, calling them both "tunicles" and prescribing their use for assisting ministers at the Eucharist. Later Anglican usage often vested a crucifer in a tunicle. Like the chasuble, both these vestments conformed to the liturgical color of the celebration.

The *cope* is in origin a cape-like variant of the chasuble, usually conforming to the liturgical color of the celebration. It may be worn over alb, surplice, or rochet by anyone—ordained or lay—with a function in public worship. English usage since 1549 has been to treat it as an alternative to the chasuble at the Eucharist, and Archbishop Parker's *Advertisements* and the Canons of 1604 require its use by the celebrant and assisting ministers at the Eucharist in cathedral and collegiate churches. The cope has come to be worn for processions and services like weddings and baptisms when celebrated without the Eucharist. It has come (with the miter) to be thought of as the proper vestment for bishops, but it is not restricted to bishops and the bishop's proper eucharistic vestment is the chasuble.

Insignia of Office. The *stole* is a long narrow band of material that is the proper insigne of office for ordained ministers. Presbyters and bishops wear it over the shoulders and hanging down in front. Usually worn over the alb or surplice, it is sometimes worn over the chasuble today, especially when a white all-purpose chasuble is used. It conforms to the liturgical color of the celebration. Presbyters have sometimes crossed the stole over their breasts and girded it in the cincture, while bishops always wear the stole uncrossed. Originally, the deacon seems to have worn the stole over the left shoulder, hanging down in front and back. In Western usage, the deacon now wears the stole with the center over the alb or surplice on the left shoulder and the ends fastened (in the cincture when the girded alb is worn) at the waist under the right arm. In Eastern usage deacons wear the stole (often broader than that used in the West) simply draped over the left shoulder in the original fashion or under the right arm with the ends brought over the left shoulder and hanging down in front and back. This style has gained recently some currency for deacons in the West also.

The *maniple* is in present form a strip of material with its two ends attached which is worn over the left wrist of the alb by ministers of the Eucharist. Originally it was a handkerchief used to signal certain actions in the rite. Since it serves no real or symbolic purpose, it has in recent decades fallen into disuse.

The bishop's *miter* is a piece of headgear that came into liturgical use in the Middle Ages. It should be treated as an insigne of office; it is in fact the only vestment which distinguishes bishop from presbyter at the Eucharist. Other insignia of office worn by the bishop include the *cross* worn on a chain about the neck which Anglican bishops have adopted in the past century and the *ring*—a signet ring in origin. The *pastoral staff* or crozier is a walking stick in the form of a shepherd's crook carried by bishops as a sign of office in liturgical functions. Archbishops may in addition have a *primatial cross* carried before them.

Academic Insignia. A *gown* worn over the cassock was academic dress in the Middle Ages. Graduates wore over this a *hood* over their backs and a *tippet,* a black scarf, over their necks and hanging down in front. Non-graduates wore only the tippet. In liturgical functions, hood and/or tippet might be worn over the surplice as well as over the gown. The English Canons of 1604 require this usage. In actual fact, gown with hood and scarf was often worn by the preacher for the sermon, and low churchmen preferred to wear this as their liturgical garb on all occasions—the Genevan practice. Today academic insignia seem irrelevant to liturgical celebration and their use is declining.

Liturgical Colors. Eucharistic vestments, stoles, maniples, copes, and hangings for altar, pulpit, and lectern have commonly followed seasonal usage. This custom fell into disuse in post-Reformation England and was generally revived there only in the last century. It is now nearly universal, though there is recently something of a return to all-purpose vestments and hangings. No usage is fixed by rubric or canon in England or here: it is a matter of tradition and custom. The following table indicates general Western usage, with notes as to variants:

Advent	purple (English, blue)
Christmas	white, gold (English, best)
Epiphany	white, gold (English, best)
Lent	purple (English, Lenten array)
Holy Week	purple (English and modern, oxblood or red)
Easter Season	white, gold (English, best)
Pentecost	red
Ordinary Time	green
Feasts of Christ	white, gold (English, best)
Feasts of Martyrs	red
Other Feasts	white
Marriage	white
Ordination	white, red (or today, seasonal)
Baptism	white (today, seasonal)
Burial	black, purple (today, white)

It is not uncommon today to have a single set of hangings (or a festal set and a Lenten set) and to change only stoles and eucharistic vestments by season. Sometimes eucharistic vestments too may be white and worn with stoles in seasonal colors. Finally, all-purpose stoles are also sometimes used today.

English Usage: Since the Reformation in England, vestments have been regulated by rubric and canon. While this has not been true in the American Episcopal Church, English custom has by and large set the precedent for American usage, and so we turn now to the provisions that have been in force in the Church of England over the centuries. These provisions are as follows:

1549 Prayer Book (The Catholic Tradition)

reinstituted by the Ornaments Rubric of the 1559 Prayer Book and all subsequent English editions

For the Eucharist
Celebrant
    plain alb
    vestment (=chasuble, stole, maniple) or cope
Assisting ministers
    plain alb
    tunicles (dalmatic and tunicle not distinguished)

For other services (Choir Vestments)
cassock and surplice
(tippet and hood for ordained graduates)
(tippet for those ordained without degree)
rochet, chimere, hood, and scarf for bishops

1552 Prayer Book (the Evangelical Tradition)

Eucharistic vestments discontinued
Choir vestments used at all times

1566 Advertisements and 1604 Canons

1552 Vestments
Cathedral and collegiate churches
    ministers of the Eucharist in copes

Nineteenth and Twentieth Centuries

1549 usage for the Catholic Tradition
1552 usage for the Evangelical Tradition
    sometimes use of the stole has been adopted

Broad Church options for the Eucharist

    cassock, surplice, and stole
    cassock, surplice, stole, and cope
    alb, stole, and white linen chasuble

Ironically, the 1559 Ornaments Rubric remained largely a dead letter in its own day (the reason for Archbishop Parker's *Advertisements* was to secure conformity to some standards, since the rubric proved unenforceable), so that there was considerable surprise and consternation when the discovery was made in the nineteenth century that the rubric in fact required the 1549, not the 1552 usage.

Recommendations for Contemporary Usage: Today's preference for simplicity leads to the recommendation that all who vest for worship wear the alb as the basic vestment for all services. Except for the Daily Office, it is appropriate that the ordained wear a stole as the sign or insigne of their office. A bishop or presbyter who presides as the principal celebrant at the Eucharist may wear a chasuble over the alb (with stole under or over the chasuble); similarly, concelebrants may wear matching or compatible chasubles. To this bishops may add the miter as distinctive of their order of ministry, particularly when performing some episcopal function (such as confirmation or ordination) in the context of the Eucharist. A bishop may also carry a simple wooden staff as a sign of office.

Deacons at the Eucharist may wear the dalmatic over alb and stole. When they wear the stole without dalmatic, it may be worn in either Western or Eastern fashion. Bishops and presbyters taking a deacon's functions in the absence of deacons should not vest as deacons: to do so diminishes the diaconate as a separate and distinct ministry. Since the subdiaconate is not a functional order of ministry today, the tunicle is a redundant vestment.

Lay persons might best be vested in alb if seated in the chancel. It is on the whole preferable, however, for readers, leaders of the intercession, (in the absence of a deacon), and perhaps even lay eucharistic ministers to come forward from the congregation to perform these functions, and so they will not be vested.

Western tradition would favor the use of the alb alone, without vestment or sign of office for the Daily Office, since functions at these services are not generally assigned to specific orders of ministry. This has not always been the case, however, and for the solemn festive Office ministers might vest in alb and stole, with dalmatics for deacons, copes for presbyters, and copes and miters for bishops. Academic insignia (such as stole and tippet) are probably best omitted with choir vestments today, except perhaps in academic settings. Bishops by long tradition might continue to wear chimere with alb or rochet.

Contemporary vestments, like ancient ones, themselves signify the order and function of those who wear them and need no ornamentation. The highly artificial symbolic rationales for vestments devised in the Middle Ages have lost their credibility today. Simpler fabrics are now preferred to brocades, and vestments depend upon texture, color, and cut for their beauty. On occasions of informal worship, vestments may at times be omitted entirely.

The Setting for Worship: The House of the Church

The Book of Common Prayer itself sets very few requirements for the building in which the congregation gathers for worship, which the early church named "the house of the church." The basic requirements arise out of the nature of the worship itself. Such a building, when used on a permanent basis for parochial worship, requires the following:

a. an altar table;

b. a lectern (ambo) and/or pulpit;

c. seats for officiating and assisting ministers;

d. a font for baptism.

These four are the focal points for worship; their location is determined by considerations of visibility and audibility. The first three are customarily placed on a platform (the chancel) together, raised a modest distance above the area where the congregation gathers (the nave). The font is customarily placed near the entrance to the church: this is the preferable location if the congregation can see and hear baptisms in this place, for Baptism is the rite of entry into the church.

A chancel platform with the congregation gathered on three of its sides is preferable to the more traditional arrangement where altar, choir, lectern and pulpit, and nave are located along a single axis in a long narrow building. In this latter arrangement, the choir becomes a visual barrier between altar and congregation and creates an undesirable sense of distance and separation. A thrust platform with the congregation on three sides creates and fosters a sense of community.

Additional requirements include the following:

e. seating for the congregation;

f. an organ (or other instrument) and seating for a choir;

g. processional space for movement in services.

We now turn to look at each of these requirements in greater detail.

The Altar Table: this is the focal point of the Celebration of the Holy Communion. It is a table and therefore should properly be freestanding, even if the celebrant does not face the congregation across it in this part of the service. Rubrics require that the table be covered "with a clean white cloth" (generally known as a fair linen) during a celebration; this usually takes the form of a runner which falls down over the two ends. Underneath the fair linen a "carpet" or frontal is customary though not required. A carpet (also known as a Jacobean or Laudian frontal) which hangs down to the floor on all four sides is perhaps the most attractive way of vesting the table. Other styles of frontal include the full frontal (which hangs down to the floor on the front only) and the superfrontal (a decorative strip of material hanging down only a few inches over the front). Two candles may be placed on the altar (allusion is made to these in services for the Dedication of a Church, the Order of Worship for the Evening, and the Great Vigil of Easter). Alternatively, processional torches or standing torches may be placed beside the altar. A stand or cushion for the altar book is also desirable. Apart from this, only the vessels for communion should be placed on the altar, these being brought there at the Offertory.

Near the altar there should be a credence shelf or table to hold communion vessels and alms basins when not in use on the altar. At the rear of the church another shelf or table will hold the bread and wine until they are brought to the altar at the Offertory. An aumbry (wall safe) near the altar is desirable to reserve consecrated bread and wine for the communion of the sick.

Reference to "altar rails" remains in the directions "Concerning the Rite" for the Reconciliation of a Penitent. Nevertheless, *The Book of Common Prayer* 1979 does not presuppose the use of altar rails for the ministration of communion. If communion is to be received kneeling, a movable railing or benches along the front aisle of the nave are preferable: it makes the rail more accessible to the congregation, allows a longer rail in many cases for more efficient ministration of communion, and does not act as a barrier between chancel and nave. Communion may also be received standing, in which case a railing is unnecessary.

The Lectern and/or Pulpit: this is the focal point for the Proclamation of the Word of God in the Eucharist and for the Ministry of the Word in other services. The lectern or ambo is used for the reading of the Scriptures and for the sermon. In the West it very soon became common to use a second ambo, the pulpit, as the gospel lectern, and to preach the sermon from this ambo as well. A single ambo will serve both purposes, however, and serves to unify this part of the service visually. The most common place for the lectern(s) is at the front of the chancel platform, on the same level as the platform or slightly raised. Other arrangements are possible, of course; in a collegiate seating arrangement the lectern may be located in the central aisle. The pulpit is often decorated with a pulpit fall in seasonal or all-purpose colors.

Seats for Officiating and Assisting Ministers: The ancient location for seating in the chancel is behind the altar in the apse. Seating on one or both sides of the space before the altar is also possible. Most episcopal services presuppose a chair placed in front of the altar from which the bishop presides until the offertory, when the chair is moved. The special bishop's chair common until recently is a useless piece of furniture, because such chairs are generally too massive to be easily moved into the position required by the rubrics of episcopal services. The chair ordinarily used by the officiant will serve quite adequately for the bishop when needed.

The Font: Our baptismal theology and practice is currently in transition, and this makes it hard to deal in complete confidence with the location and nature of the font. Ancient baptistries were designed for the baptism of adults, who went naked into a shallow pool, were baptized with water poured over them, and were clothed in clean white tunics to be presented to the church assembled for the Eucharist. This manner of baptism required a special chamber and dressing rooms as well. For modesty's sake, the actual baptism was not performed in the sight of the congregation. Although once again adult baptism is understood as the normative rite and immersion is the preferred means of administering the sacrament, it is unlikely that we will return to the custom of baptizing candidates naked. It is therefore possible to place the font or pool within the church near the entrance. A shallow pool with running water could be used for the partial immersion of adults customary in the ancient church; a substantial standing font would serve for the immersion of infants, if desired, and baptism of adults by affusion (pouring).

In some of our present churches, a location near the entrance is not possible if baptisms are to be in full sight of the congregation. A font near the entrance also must not block processional space or make it difficult to bring in a coffin for burial. Another possible, though less desirable, location, is at the front of the chancel platform. Often churches have both lectern and pulpit; one of these might serve for both reading and preaching and the font might be moved into the place of the other.

Seating for the Congregation: Seating for the congregation did not come into general use until the very end of the Middle Ages. We now have come to expect it. Wooden chairs, however, are preferable for this purpose to fixed pews. The nave, the area of congregational seating, has for most of Christian history been a multipurpose space, and it can best serve in this way if it has movable rather than fixed seating. If possible, as we noted above, seating should be arranged around three sides of the chancel and altar, with the congregation facing each other across the chancel. In a long narrow space, the collegiate style of seating, where the congregation face each other across a broad central aisle (with altar table, lectern, and seats for officiants and assistants arranged in this aisle) is preferable to the more usual arrangement.

The Organ (or other instrument) and Choir Seating: Acoustical considerations are of first importance in the placement of musical instrument and choir seating. Choir and instrument need to be close to each other; an organ needs to speak out into the nave and not be muffled in a side chamber; and the choir needs to be in a position to lead congregational singing. The customary location in a divided chancel between altar and nave has problems, as we have noted above. Possibilities include seating the choir behind the altar (in redesign of traditional chancels), placing them to one side of the chancel platform when the congregation sits on three sides of the platform, or placing them at the front or rear of the nave seating. The use of a rear gallery for the choir separates them from the altar and the congregation and from the action of the liturgy.

Processional Space: Except for the Daily Office, most services of *The Book of Common Prayer* are processional in nature—that is, they call for the movement of groups of people during the course of the service. The church needs to be laid out to facilitate this movement, with a wide center aisle and (in most cases) front, back, and side aisles.

Chapel Space: Most parishes could also use a smaller space designed for the Daily Office and weekday Eucharists. This may be an entirely separate space, or it may open onto the main church. Its foci should be altar, lectern, and seating for officiants and assistants; it may prove wise to have all furniture and seating movable, so that the space may be configured in different ways.

The house of the church should be designed as a setting for the worship of the church. In other words, its design should be functional. In the last century, churches were generally built to create a numinous atmosphere; the liturgy had to be accommodated to the building. Such buildings were generally created in Gothic revival style—long and narrow. Even churches built in other styles tended to keep the long, narrow layout of the Gothic building. Unfortunately, such buildings do not work well as a setting for the services of *The Book of Common Prayer*; they work against a sense of community, and they often present visual and acoustical problems. Such buildings need to be readapted, as far as possible, for the services of the Prayer Book; new buildings should be built to a more functional design.

Ceremonial Action

Ceremonial actions are the "body language" of Christian worship; they are best understood as functional actions and rhetorical gestures which draw out the meaning of liturgical prayer. In the words of the section entitled "Of Ceremonies" in the 1549 Prayer Book, they should be "so set forth that every man may understand what they do mean, and to what use they do serve." This section goes on to prescribe as "touching...gestures: they may be used or left as every man's devotion serveth without blame." Officiants, of course, need to take into consideration the "devotion" of the congregation as well as their own.

Over the course of time ceremonial actions tend to accumulate and clutter liturgical rites, distorting their structure, proportion, and meaning. In the Middle Ages a fascination with allegory and a highly artificial symbolism developed which had a pernicious effect on Christian worship. The English reformers "pruned" the ceremony of the Prayer Book with considerable skill, but the spare ceremony of the Prayer Book rites led nineteenth-century Anglicans to impose on the Prayer Book the ceremonial tradition of the Roman Rite. Two problems arise from this:

1. The ceremonial of the Roman Rite does not always conform to the structure, rationale, and theology of Anglican rites;

2. The Roman Rite before the reforms of the Second Vatican Council retained the mediaeval stratum noted above, to the detriment of the liturgy.

In particular, this ceremonial of the Roman Rite poses problems when imposed on Anglican Eucharistic Prayers. It is inappropriate because the structure of the Roman Canon is different from that of Eucharistic Prayers in the Scottish-American tradition. It is also inappropriate because it presupposes a theology of consecration alien to Anglicans.

The notes which follow are offered to assist in "reading" the meaning of common ceremonial postures, gestures, actions, and uses, and in selecting those that are appropriate for contemporary Episcopal worship. The Catholic tradition will favor a fuller ceremonial usage and the Evangelical tradition a sparer one, but when the usage conforms to the requirements of functional action and rhetorical gesture, it meets the standards of Anglican worship.

Standing is the normal posture for prayer in Christian tradition, for we have been "raised" with Christ. Standing is also the customary posture for praise, affirmation of faith, and respect for the Gospel at the Eucharist.

Kneeling is the customary posture for prayers of penitence and confession and prayers of fervent supplication. In recent centuries, the celebrant or officiant has kept to the custom of standing, while the congregation has in general knelt for prayer. In *The Book of Common Prayer* 1979, kneeling is appropriate for the Confession and the Prayer of Humble Access and perhaps the Prayers of the People. When a special posture is particularly appropriate during a service, rubrics generally specify it. When two postures are legitimate options, both are given; the first given is usually preferable.

Sitting is appropriate for hearing lessons (except the Gospel at the Eucharist) and sermons and also for psalmnody between lessons.

Arms outstretched, palms raised is the *orans* position, a classic Christian gesture of prayer. Hands are stretched out to God, ready to receive what God gives. Today, the celebrant or officiant uses this gesture customarily for prayers said on behalf of the congregation.

Folded or clasped hands is a later gesture of prayer. In origin the folded hands probably derive from a gesture of feudal loyalty: one placed the folded hands within the hands of one's liege lord as a sign of obedience. The celebrant or officiant usually uses this gesture for prayers said in unison with the congregation or prayers said by others; others use it for all prayers. Clasped hands look more natural than folded hands. Officiants in worship generally also keep the hands clasped when not otherwise occupied.

A bow is a gesture of respect. A simple bow of the head is a gesture of respect to the name of Jesus or of the Trinity, to the altar, to the cross, and to persons. A solemn bow from the waist (sometimes replaced by a simple bow) is a gesture of respect to Christ present in the sacrament, to Christ in his incarnation (in the Creed), and to the altar on entering and leaving the Church. A genuflection is sometimes used for the solemn bow in Catholic ceremonial. It should not be used behind the altar. A simple bow should replace both the solemn bow and genuflection when one is carrying something (other than a book) in one's hands.

Hands opened is a gesture of greeting and invitation, generally used with the salutation and other greetings and invitations.

The celebrant or officiant customarily begins prayer by opening the hands in invitation, either at the salutation or at the bidding, "Let us pray." Hands may then be closed again to draw the congregation into the prayer. The celebrant then continues in the orans position, bows the head for the name of Jesus (and the doxology) at the end of the prayer, closing the hands to draw the congregation into the Amen. During prayer, for grace of gesture, the celebrant closes the hands if the head is bowed.

Hands laid on objects or persons is a sign of the Spirit invoked in blessing, dedication, or absolution.

Hands extended over objects or persons is a similar sign of the invocation of the Spirit.

The sign of the cross is made over objects or persons as a sign of blessing or absolution. It is a more recent gesture for this than the two gestures above, which Evangelicals often prefer to substitute for it. One makes the sign on oneself as a gesture of blessing or absolution received and as a seal of faith at the beginning and end of services or prayer. Its use with the Creed might be thought of as a memorial of baptism. Its use at the beginning of the Gospel and Gospel canticles apparently is to be read as expressing the desire to secure for oneself the blessings of the Gospel. It has come to be used at the end of the Gloria in excelsis, but it is hard to put forth any compelling rationale for its use there. It is sometimes made during the Benedictus qui venit of the Sanctus, but this is probably a mistaken reading of the meaning of this text: the one "who comes in the name of the Lord" here is probably Christ, not the worshiper. The sign should not be unnecessarily multiplied or rushed: to do either trivializes the gesture. Mystical multiples such as three (for the persons of the trinity), five (for the wounds of Christ), and so on are arbitrary and unconvincing and best avoided.

Hands lifted at the bidding, "Lift up your hearts" is a natural gesture.

Objects lifted up are offered to God. This gesture should ordinarily be related to words such as "offer" or "present" in the texts of prayers.

A kiss is a gesture of greeting and respect. It has been customary for the celebrant to kiss the altar on approaching it at the beginning of the service and on departing from it at the end of the service and to kiss the Gospel book after the Gospel has been read. This custom seems culturally alien in American society and is generally omitted today.

The peace was once given in the form of a kiss as a sign of greeting and reconciliation. Today, a handclasp or embrace are more common gestures at the peace.

The Use of Lights: Candles are often used as ornaments to set off focal points of the church such as the altar, the lectern, and the font. They may also be carried in procession. They have no particular theological meaning here but are rather a sign of festivity, much as they are in our homes. In earlier times they were considered significant by those in the Catholic tradition, who favored their use (often in arcane mystical multiples), and those in the Evangelical tradition, who violently opposed their use. They are customary in most places today. They should ordinarily be lit and extinguished unobtrusively in services.

At times, the lighting or extinguishing of candles does have a particular meaning. In such cases the meaning is generally related to the theme of Christ as the light of the world. Lighting of the Paschal Candle at the Easter Vigil, of candles at the Order of Worship for the Evening, and of the Wreath at Advent services is related to this theme;

the presentation of a candle to the newly baptized is meant to emphasize the meaning of baptism as enlightenment; and the extinguishing of candles at tenebrae is meant to emphasize the darkness of Christ's absence.

The Use of Incense: This is perhaps the most controversial of the ceremonial practices considered, and *The Book of Common Prayer* 1979 is the first edition of the Prayer Book to refer to it (in the "Additional Directions" of the Order of Worship for the Evening and for the Consecration of a Church). Its use calls for considerable pastoral sensitivity, and it should be omitted if it proves divisive or offensive. Incense may be understood to represent the prayers of the saints (its apparent meaning when used during the last canticle of Morning or Evening Prayer), our prayers, a blessing, or a sign of respect. Censing should never be so elaborate or intrusive as to distort or obscure the main structure and meaning of a service.

The simplest use is processional: in the entrance procession at the Eucharist and certain other services and at the Gospel procession. It might also be burned to represent our prayers or the prayers of the saints at the Office canticles, at the Phos hilaron, and during the Great Thanksgiving.

A somewhat fuller use would incense objects as well—the altar and eucharistic gifts at the Offertory, the altar during the last office canticle and Phos Hilaron, the Gospel Book before the Gospel is read, and objects to be blessed as appropriate. The altar is also customarily censed at the entrance procession in the Eucharist, but this censing might best be omitted if it is to be censed at the Offertory. Similarly, one should choose either the Phos hilaron or the Gospel canticle for censing the altar at the Evening Office, but not both.

The fullest use would cense persons as well as objects. They are perhaps best censed in groups—those in the chancel first and then the congregation. This censing customarily follows the censing of the altar at the Offertory at the Eucharist and during the Office. Once again, the censing should be simple and unobtrusive; elaborate patterns are to be avoided. It is perhaps best to cense persons and objects by swinging the censer toward them, and to cense the altar by walking around it while swinging the censer. The Catholic tradition favors the use of incense, the Evangelical tradition avoids it; Anglican tradition as a whole uses it with caution and restraint. A similar range of usage is found among Lutherans.

The Language of the Liturgy

The standard language of *The Book of Common Prayer* 1979 is contemporary English. However, forms of Morning and Evening Prayer, the Eucharist, and the Burial Office have also been provided in the traditional language of the sixteenth century, and these are known as Rite One Services. The rubrics on page 14 of the 1979 Prayer Book further provide:

> *In any of the Proper Liturgies for Special Days, and in other services contained in this Book celebrated in the context of a Rite One service, the contemporary idiom may be conformed to traditional language.*

> *When it is desired to use music composed for them, previously authorized liturgical texts may be used in place of the corresponding texts in this Book.*

These provisions show pastoral sensitivity and a concern to conserve the cultural heritage of our Anglican past.

However, the Church followed the proper instinct in making contemporary English (Rite Two) the standard language of the book. In its day, the traditional language of Rite One was the contemporary idiom, and that was the reason it was used for worship.

The Use of Music

The rubrics of particular services indicate in the 1979 Prayer Book where hymns and anthems are appropriate. A rubric on page 14 specifies what is meant by the words "hymn" and "anthem."

> *Hymns referred to in the rubrics of this Book are to be understood as those authorized by this Church. The words of anthems are to be from Holy Scripture, or from this Book or from texts congruent with them.*

It should be noted that the general rubric of prior Books authorizing hymns and anthems before and after services and sermons has been withdrawn. If a hymn or anthem is appropriate, the rubrics of a service say so.

All texts from the Prayer Book may be sung or said. Another rubric on page 14 states:

> *Where rubrics indicate that a part of a service is to be "said", it must be understood to include "or sung" and vice versa.*

In actual fact, the rubrics often indicate a preference for singing a text. Such texts include:

a. Psalms at the Office, in the Eucharist, and in other services;

b. the invitatory psalms, canticle, and hymn (Phos hilaron), and the Office canticles;

c. the Kyrie eleison, Trisagion, Gloria in excelsis (or canticle used in its place), Sanctus/Benedictus and Agnus Dei at the Eucharist, along with the dialogue and Preface;

d. anthems—at the fraction in the Eucharist (confractoria), at the candle lighting in the Order of Worship for the Evening (lucernaria), in the Proper Liturgies for Holy Week, and at entrance, commendation, and committal in the Burial of the Dead;

e. the Exsultet and the Alleluia of the Great Vigil of Easter.

Beyond this, how much of a service is sung or said is a matter of personal or parochial preference, pastoral sensitivity, and the musical ability of congregation, officiants, and musicians. Some texts, of course, do not readily lend themselves to singing: confessions and absolutions, examinations and exhortations, and questions and answers are obvious examples. The initial Anglican practice can be seen in the fact that John Merbecke's 1550 *Book of Common Prayer*

Noted presumes that almost the entire text of the Daily Office and the Eucharist will be sung.

Catholic preference is for the full sung services; Evangelicals on the whole prefer a said service apart from hymns, canticles, psalms, and anthems. Contemporary usage tends to prefer reading the lessons of the Office and the Eucharist to singing them. The service music of the Hymnal, supplemented by *The Altar Book, Music for Ministers and Congregations,* the *Gradual Psalms,* and forthcoming psalters provide resources for singing whatever parts of the service are desired. We will take note of these provisions in considering individual services.

A final musical provision of the 1979 Book is the direction giving permission to use instrumental music:

> *On occasion, and as appropriate, instrumental music may be substituted for a hymn or anthem.*

CHAPTER 2

The Daily Office

Daily Morning and Evening Prayer are part of the *regular* public worship of the church, intended (as the title indicates) for *daily* use. In some situations, worship at noontime and bedtime may also be appropriate, and for these occasions the orders for Noonday Prayer and Compline are provided for optional use. For a festive form of Evening Prayer an Order of Worship for the Evening is included. Daily Devotions for Families and Individuals are informal versions of these Offices. All share a common basic structure:

> **The (Invitatory and) Psalter**
> **The Lesson(s)**
> **The Prayers**

The Church gathers, as the invitation to confession in Morning Prayer, Rite I (page 41), says "to set forth [God's] most worthy praise, to hear his holy Word, and to ask, for ourselves and on behalf of others, those things that are necessary for our life and our salvation." To this basic structure the orders for Morning and Evening Prayer and for Compline provide a penitential introduction for use as desired, and

Morning and Evening Prayer also provide for additional devotional material at the conclusion. Praise, Scripture, and Prayer are offered as the proper daily diet of Christians. Morning and Evening Prayer are provided in both traditional and contemporary language.

The Participants

Early forms of the Office presumed an assembly of the Church in its various orders and assigned appropriate functions for each order. Some monastic Offices (since early monks were all lay persons) omitted litanies and prayers, as appropriate only for deacons and for bishops or presbyters, using in their place the Kyrie eleison (the response to the litany) and the Lord's Prayer.

The Prayer Book, in conformity to later use in the West, states in the rubrics on pages 36 and 74:

> *In the Daily Office, the term "Officiant" is used to denote the person, clerical or lay, who leads the Office.*

> *It is appropriate that other persons be assigned to read the Lessons, and to lead other parts of the service not assigned to the officiant. The bishop, when present, appropriately concludes the Office with a blessing.*

The Order of Worship for the Evening, in this as in other things reflecting earlier usage, does set out appropriate functions for all orders of ministry in the rubric on page 108:

> *Any part or parts of this service may be led by lay persons. A priest [= presbyter] or deacon, when presiding, should read the Prayer for Light, and the Blessing or Dismissal at the end. The bishop, when present, should give the Blessing.*

Stricter adherence to tradition would have a bishop or presbyter preside when present, would assign psalter collects to presbyters, and would have a deacon lead the litany of the Office and give the dismissal. Functions would be assigned in a similar way at Morning and Evening Prayer.

Vestments

For the weekday parochial Office, it might be appropriate to omit vestments on informal occasions. Otherwise it is appropriate for officiants and choir to vest in alb (or cassock and surplice). The custom of wearing academic insignia (tippet and hood) is perhaps best abandoned, for they have no explicitly religious significance. For festal Morning and Evening Prayer on Sundays and feasts, it would be appropriate for bishops and presbyters with specific functions to add stole and cope (and miter for bishops) and for deacons to add to the alb stole and dalmatic. A lay officiant at the festal Office also might wear cope over alb (or cassock and surplice).

Music

The choir Office has been a strong tradition in Anglicanism from the time of the Reformation, particularly in cathedral and collegiate churches. The Hymnal provides complete music for the choral rendition of the entire Office (except for the penitential introduction). For the psalter, it is necessary to provide pointed texts for the plainsong tones or Anglican Chant tunes in the Hymnal, or to use a complete psalter (*The Anglican Chant Psalter* is now in print). In the ordinary parish church, the Office will generally be said on weekdays, but may be sung on Sundays and feasts.

The Meaning of Incense at the Office

Juan Mateos ("The Origins of the Divine Office", *Worship,* Vol. 41, 1967, pp. 477–485; "The Morning and Evening Office", *Worship,* Vol. 42, 1968, pp. 31–47) and Gabriele Winkler ("Über die Kathedralvesper in den verschiedenen Riten des Ostens und Westens", *Archiv für die Liturgiewissenschaft,* Vol. 16, 1974, pp. 53–102) trace the ultimate origin of the use of incense at the morning and evening Office to Exodus 30, which mandates the morning and evening oblation of incense in the temple. Exodus 29 legislates the daily offering of a lamb at the same times, and these temple sacrifices set the times for the synagogue services from which the Christian Offices derive. Patristic authors refer to these passages, and they are the apparent source for the description of these Offices as "legitimae orationes," "times of prayer prescribed by the law." (Tertullian: *On Prayer,* Chapter 25; and John Chrysostom: *Commentary on Psalm 140:3.*) The more immediate source for the custom of burning incense would have been the Jewish domestic offering of incense when lights were kindled on Sabbaths and festivals. It is in fact in connection with the lamplighting ceremony at the evening Office that we first find mention of the offering of incense.

The meaning of the oblation of incense would seem to lie in the rising smoke as a sign of prayer "set forth in [God's] sight as the incense," mingled with the prayers of the saints (Revelation). At times such prayers are strongly marked as prayers of penitence: Psalm 141 is sometimes understood in this way, and Psalm 51 is sometimes used as a text with the offering of incense. Juan Mateos sees the use of incense in the Roman Rite during the Benedictus Dominus and the Magnificat as representative of the prayers of the saints.

With this meaning, it would seem appropriate to offer incense before the altar at Morning Prayer and Evening Prayer, rather than to cense the altar and the people.

Ceremonial Traditions

Variants among the ceremonial traditions of Anglicanism at the Office concern primarily the use of gestures, the use of incense, and (to a lesser extent) how much of the Office is sung. Those in the Catholic tradition will use the sign of the cross when indicated in directions for the Office below, while Evangelicals may wish to substitute another gesture (as at absolution and blessing) or omit it. Catholics may wish to use, and Evangelicals to avoid, incense. Evangelicals will probably prefer to say rather than sing the lessons, the Creed, and the Lord's Prayer, and perhaps all the Prayers. In terms of vestments, Evangelicals will use only the basic vestments (alb or cassock and surplice). The strict Anglican tradition is comfortable with these variants, which are not great in any case.

Morning Prayer
and Evening Prayer

Preparations

Lessons should be marked in the lectern Bible or Office Readings.
Altar and/or Pavement Candles and candles at the lectern may be lit
(except when the Order of Worship for the Evening is used).
Officiants (and choir) enter in a silent procession. The rubrics provide
no hymn for entrance or departure (unlike the general rubrics of
previous Prayer Books) and none is intended. If incense is to be used,
the censer (thurible) should be prepared. The officiant and assistants
preside from the chancel seating.

Introductory Material

Opening Sentences, general and seasonal, are provided. The officiant
may begin with the sentence and continue with the invitation,
confession, and absolution; or go from the sentence directly to the
preces; or begin at once with the preces. The opening sentence is said
if it precedes the penitential order; it may be sung on a monotone if
the officiant continues at once with the preces. All stand when the
officiant enters, or when the officiant (if already seated before the
service) rises to begin the service.

If the penitential order is used, the officiant then turns to the
congregation and uses the longer or shorter form of the *invitation to
confession. Silence* appropriately follows, and all kneel (or bow, if
kneeling is awkward) and join in the *confession.* A bishop or presbyter
then rises and says the *absolution,* making the sign of the cross over
the people or stretching a hand over them. Deacons and lay persons
when presiding alter the wording of the absolution as indicated in the
rubric, remain kneeling, and may (if they wish) sign themselves with
the cross. The Penitential Order might perhaps be used during Lent
and on other days of special devotion listed in the Prayer Book on
page 17. It might be omitted at other times.

The Invitatory and the Psalter

This section is the beginning of the Office proper. All stand, or remain standing, for the *preces*. "Alleluia" is omitted in Lent and in Rite I may be omitted at other times also. Music for the preces is provided in the Hymnal at S 1 and S 26 (Morning Prayer and Evening Prayer, Rite I) and at S 33 and S 60 (Morning Prayer and Evening Prayer, Rite II). It is customary Catholic usage to sign oneself with the cross at the beginning of the preces (or to sign one's lips at Morning Prayer). Here and elsewhere it is customary to bow the head as a sign of respect for the Trinity at the Gloria Patri. At Morning Prayer *an invitatory psalm*—Psalm 95 in part or in full or Psalm 100—follows (music at S 2–15, Rite I; S 34–45, Rite II). *The Easter Canticle* replaces the invitatory during Easter week and may be used in place of the invitatory throughout Easter Season (music at S 16–20, Rite I; S 46–50, Rite II). Invitatory antiphons or refrains are provided which may be used before and after the psalms, or used for a responsorial rendition of them (Accompaniment Edition of the Hymnal, S 289–292, Rite I; S 293–294, Rite II). The refrain for the Easter Canticle is "Alleluia," printed in the text of the canticle. It is unfortunate that the antiphons are not printed in the Singers' Edition of the Hymnal, for this is the very part that the congregation needs in responsorial rendition! If not sung responsorially, the psalms and canticle may be sung either by all together or antiphonally. The Gloria Patri may be sung with the invitatory psalms and canticle or omitted. Metrical versions of the invitatory psalms are permitted by rubric and may be found as Hymn 395 (Psalm 95) and Hymns 377, 378, and 391 (Psalm 100).

At Evening Prayer, an *Office hymn* normally follows the preces, though it may be omitted. The ancient lamplighting hymn Phos hilaron is printed in the text of the service. Music for the prose text is found in the Hymnal at S 27 (Rite I) and S 59–61 (Rite II). Metrical versions are found as Hymns 25, 26, 36, and 37. Other hymns may be used in place of the Phos hilaron. Such hymns should properly be hymns for the evening, for the feast, or for the season; they need not necessarily be the traditional Latin Office hymns. The invitatory psalms or canticle from Morning Prayer may also be used in place of the Office hymn. Incense may be burned or the altar (and people, if desired) censed during the Office hymn, though the customary Western usage is to do this during the last canticle (the Magnificat).

The Psalm or Psalms appointed for the Office are listed in the Daily Office Lectionary. The lectionary distributes the psalms over a seven-week course, with seasonal variations. The morning psalms are listed first, the evening psalms second. The rubric provides (page 934):

> *At the discretion of the officiant, however, any of the Psalms appointed for a given day may be used in the morning or in the evening. Likewise, Psalms appointed for any day may be used on any other day in the same week, except on major Holy Days.*

This provision should be used with caution, however, to avoid using a distinctly morning psalm in the evening or vice versa. The psalms for Fridays (usually Passion or Penitential Psalms) and for Saturdays and Sundays (usually psalms of creation or paschal deliverance) are also particularly appropriate to those days and should be changed only with great caution. A further rubric (page 935) provides:

> *Brackets and parentheses are used (brackets in the case of whole Psalms, parentheses in the case of verses) to indicate Psalms and verses of Psalms which may be omitted. In some instances, the entire portion of the Psalter assigned to a given Office has been bracketed, and alternative Psalmody provided. Those who desire to recite the Psalter in its entirety should, in each instance, use the bracketed Psalms rather than the alternatives.*

The text of the Psalter itself also has headings for the monthly division of the Psalter traditional since 1549 and presumably this course may also be used, though no rubric deals with it. During the season of Lent the word "Hallelujah" may be omitted when it appears in the text of a psalm. A rubric in the Additional Directions for the Office (page 141) provides:

> *Gloria Patri is always sung or said at the conclusion of the entire portion of the Psalter; and may be used . . . after each Psalm, and after each section of Psalm 119.*

The psalms are traditionally recited standing in the Anglican office; sometimes, however, they are recited seated. The first alternative treats them as acts of praise; the second, following monastic tradition, as texts for meditation.

The psalms may be sung to plainsong tones (given at S 446 in the Accompaniment Edition of the Hymnal). Anglican Chants may also be used, either the tunes found at S 417–445 in the Accompaniment Edition of the Hymnal or those provided with the psalm texts in *The Anglican Chant Psalter.* Congregations will need pointed texts and the tone or tune or a copy of *The Anglican Chant Psalter* for these methods. Psalms may also be sung to Simplified Anglican Chant tunes (S 408–415, Accompaniment Edition); in this case, pointed texts are useful, but the psalms can be sung from the Psalter without pointed texts. The *Lutheran Book of Worship* has adopted our Psalter, and it would be possible to sing the psalms using the pointing in that psalter with the Lutheran tones.

Various styles of recitation are possible. Antiphonal recitation, alternating between two sides of the congregation, is the traditional style for Office Psalms. Or the psalms may be said or sung in full by all together. With Anglican Chant or Simplified Anglican Chant, an effective variation is to alternate between harmonized verses by the choir and unison verses by the congregation (the entire single or double chant should be sung through before alternating). The same variation is possible with faux bourdons on plainsong tones. When the psalms are said, responsive recitation, alternating between leader and congregation is also possible, though perhaps less satisfactory. Responsorial recitation with the use of a refrain or antiphon (see below) is a final possibility, though in Western usage this is traditional only for the invitatory psalm at the Office.

Antiphons may be used with the psalms, according to one of the Additional Directions (page 141):

> *Antiphons drawn from the Psalms themselves, or from the opening sentences given in the Offices, or from other passages of Scripture may be used with the Psalms and biblical Canticles.*

Howard Galley's *Prayer Book Office* suggests appropriate antiphons. In antiphonal recitation, the antiphon precedes and follows the psalm. In responsorial recitation, it is recited first by the leader, cantor, or choir; repeated by all; and then repeated after each verse or group of verses by all. The rubrics do not provide for metrical versions of the appointed psalms (apart from the invitatory psalm).

Additional Note on the Lectionary: On occasion, two sets of propers may be provided in the Lectionary for the same day because of a conflict in the calendar. Rules of precedence found in the Calendar of the Prayer Book will determine which Office propers are used and whether the others are transferred or omitted altogether. It should be noted that occasions listed in Category 5 in the Calendar, "Days of Optional Observance," have no Office propers. Howard Galley puts this information in tabular form on page xx of his *Prayer Book Office*. A related problem occurs when the Daily Office provides psalms and lessons for Evening Prayer on the Eve of a Sunday or feast, and that falls on the day of another Sunday or feast. This is known as the *concurrence of feasts* and the Prayer Book rubrics do not deal with that. In this case, one has to work from the apparent intent of the Prayer Book rubrics regarding precedence. Howard Galley provides rules for this, and also presents them in tabular form, on pages xix and xxi of *The Prayer Book Office*. To secure continuity in the readings, a rubric on page 934 provides:

> *When a Major Feast interrupts the sequence of Readings, they may be re-ordered by lengthening, combining, or omitting some of them, to secure continuity or avoid repetition.*

> *Any Reading may be lengthened at discretion. Suggested lengthenings are shown in parentheses.*

The Lesson(s)

The Daily Office Lectionary provides a two-year cycle of readings. Three lessons are provided for each day: an Old Testament reading, a New Testament reading, and a Gospel. The recommended usage is two lessons at Morning Prayer, and one lesson at Evening Prayer. At

Morning Prayer the Old Testament reading is read, together with the New Testament reading in Year One and the Gospel in Year Two. At Evening Prayer, the Gospel is read in Year One, the New Testament reading in Year Two. If an Old Testament reading is desired at Evening Prayer, it is borrowed from the lectionary of the alternate year. When lessons are provided for Evening Prayer on the Eve of a feast or Sunday, an Old Testament reading is provided. It is also provided for Palm Sunday and Easter Day. At certain other times, three lessons are provided for Morning Prayer. Ordinarily, three lessons may also be read at either Morning or Evening Prayer, if only one of these Offices is used each day. Formulas for introducing and concluding the lessons are given in the rubrics in the text of the service. Chapter and verse citations are probably useful only when the congregation will be following the lessons in their own Bibles. Those who desire to sing the lessons may use the directions found in *The Altar Book* or *Music for Ministers and Congregations* for lessons before the Gospel at the Eucharist. A period of *silence* is appropriate after each lesson.

A *canticle* follows the first (and second) reading. In the Anglican Office, canticles function as responses to the lessons. This usage was introduced by Archbishop Cranmer. Traditionally, Old Testament canticles and some New Testament canticles have been treated as part of the psalmody, while the Gospel canticles and prose hymns such as the Gloria in excelsis and the Te Deum are independent elements in the Office. A table on pages 144 and 145 gives a suggested usage for the canticles, but any canticle may be used after either the first or second lesson in Morning or Evening Prayer. Rite II canticles may be used with Rite I and vice versa. Some may wish to follow the older practice of using the Benedictus Dominus as the last canticle of Morning Prayer daily (except when it is suggested as the first canticle and the Te Deum as the second). Before the Reformation, it was an independent element in the Office, rather than a response to the lessons, and was treated at times as an incense song and linked by its reference to the "dayspring" or "dawn" to the theme of the Office as an act of worship at daybreak. The usage of prior Prayer Books has been to use the Magnificat and Nunc Dimittis daily at Evening Prayer, and some may wish to continue this usage when two lessons are read daily. Music for the canticles is found in the Hymnal at S 177–288. Additional settings are given in the Accompaniment Edition at S 393–407. The rubrics permit the use of an antiphon or refrain (except with the Gloria in excelsis and the Te Deum), and many canticle settings in the Hymnal include antiphons. Other antiphons may be found in Howard Galley's *Prayer Book Office*. When the Gloria Patri is printed with the text of a canticle in the Prayer Book, rubrics permit it to be used or omitted. Metrical versions of the canticles, permitted by rubric, are listed in the Hymnal on page 680 of the Accompaniment Edition, Vol. 1. When three lessons are used at one Office, no canticle follows the third reading (the Gospel). The canticles are sung or said standing.

In accordance with traditional Western usage, incense may be burned or the altar (and people, if desired) censed during the last canticle of Morning or Evening Prayer. Juan Mateos believes that here the incense represents the prayers of the saints. It may also be that the usage stems from the treatment of Gospel canticles in the same way as the Gospel at the Eucharist. It is usual to confine the use of incense to occasions when the Office is solemnly sung on Sundays and feasts.

It is also customary to sign oneself with the cross at the beginning of Gospel canticles in the same way as at the Gospel at the Eucharist.

According to the Additional Directions a *sermon* may be preached after the readings, or "*a reading from non-biblical Christian literature may follow the biblical Readings*" (page 142). The rubrics are not absolutely clear here; presumably the sermon or other reading would follow the last canticle if one or two biblical readings were used at the Office, and would follow the Gospel if three readings were used. This is the preferable place for a sermon related to the lessons. The other reading might be the biography from *Lesser Feasts and Fasts* on a major feast or on a commemoration listed on the calendar, or an appropriate patristic commentary or homily, as in the Office of Readings in current Roman Catholic use. Howard Galley provides a selection of such readings for some feasts in *The Prayer Book Office*.

The *Apostles' Creed* follows and concludes this section of the Office. All stand for it and may face liturgical East (towards the altar). One of the Additional Directions provides (page 142):

> The Apostles' Creed is omitted from the Office when the Eucharist with its own Creed is to follow. It may also be omitted at one of the Offices on weekdays.

The Creed may be said, or sung on a monotone.

The Prayers

The rubrics at the beginning of this section in the Office indicate that the people stand or kneel for the Prayers. While the rubric comes before the salutation, it would seem that, if the people are to kneel, they should do so after the bidding, "Let us pray." Local custom will determine which posture for prayer is used. Some might wish to follow the regulation of the Council of Nicea and stand on Sundays and feasts and their eves and during Easter Season and kneel at other times. The officiant should stand for the collects in this section, whichever posture is adopted for the people. The customary gestures for prayer noted in Chapter 1 should be used, though the officiant will of necessity omit them if holding a book in the hands. The prayers may be led from the officiants' seating or (especially in festive forms of the Office) from a position in the center of the chancel before the altar. The rubrics specify that the officiant lead all of the prayers in this section, except the suffrages. These are simply printed as versicles and responses or (in Suffrages B at Evening Prayer) with the response in italics. As the officiant is properly a bishop or presbyter in ancient tradition, so the leader of intercessions is properly a deacon, and leading the suffrages at the Office would be an appropriate function for the deacon, if one be present. Otherwise another presbyter, a lay person (or cantor), or the officiant might lead them.

The officiant turns to the people for the *salutation,* spreading the hands, then joining them for the *Lord's Prayer,* said with the people. There is also precedent, however, for the officiant to lead the Lord's Prayer in the orans position, with hands spread. The Lord's Prayer will be omitted if the Litany or the Eucharist follows immediately. Music for the salutation, bidding, and Lord's Prayer is found in the Hymnal at S 21, S 28, S 51, and S 62 (Morning Prayer and Evening Prayer, Rites I and II). The *Suffrages* follow. Suffrages A at Morning and Evening Prayer are the traditional Office suffrages in the Prayer Book tradition, somewhat revised. They might be used at Morning Prayer, except when the Gloria in excelsis or the Te Deum is used as the final canticle. In the latter case, Suffrages B might be used at Morning Prayer, since they are the suffrages traditionally associated with these two canticles. At Evening Prayer, Suffrages B might be the preferable alternative. These are the dismissal litany in the Byzantine tradition and make a fitting evening intercession. Music for the suffrages is found in the Hymnal at S 22 and 52 (set A for both Morning and Evening Prayer, Rites I and II), at S 23 and 53 (set B for Morning Prayer, Rites I and II) and at S 29–30 and 63–64 (set B for Evening Prayer, Rites I and II).

The Prayers conclude with *one or more collects* and (unless a general intercession such as the Great Litany or else the Eucharist follows) *one of three prayers for mission* printed in the text of each Office. Seven collects are printed with each Office, including three that are designated for Sunday, Friday, and Saturday. The other four in each Office might each be assigned to one of the other days of the week. On Sundays and feasts and their eves and during the seasons of Advent, Christmas, Lent, and Easter the collect of the day might precede the collect of the day of the week. From Christmas Eve through the Sunday after Epiphany, from the eve of Palm Sunday through the Second Sunday of Easter, and on the feasts of the Ascension, Pentecost, the Presentation, the Annunciation, the Visitation, the Nativity of St. John the Baptist, St. Peter and St. Paul, the Transfiguration, St. Mary the Virgin, the Holy Cross, St. Michael and All Angels, and All Saints the collect for the day of the week might be omitted. This usage is that recommended by Howard Galley in *The Prayer Book Office*. The third prayer for mission at Morning Prayer is particularly appropriate for Fridays and the season of Lent. Tones for singing the collects are found in the Accompaniment Edition of the

Hymnal at S 447 and S 448. Notes with the suffrages in the Accompaniment Edition indicate which tone is appropriate for which setting of the suffrages. Or the collects may be monotoned. The prayer for mission (which will be sung in the same way) concludes this section and the Office proper.

Concluding Devotions

Provision for a *hymn or anthem* at this place in the Office has been made since the time of Elizabeth I. Much of the great English church music was written for use here. A hymn for the morning or evening, the feast, or the season is also appropriate. On feasts the Office might be concluded with *a procession to a suitable station* during this hymn, ending with a versicle and response, an appropriate collect, the dismissal, and the sentence. Such processions are traditionally begun with the deacon's bidding, "Let us go forth in peace," to which the people respond, "In the name of Christ. Amen." Music for this may be found in the Hymnal with the music for Palm Sunday at Hymn 153. On baptismal feasts, the station might be the font and the collect *a memorial of baptism,* as Howard Galley suggests in *The Prayer Book Office,* on the basis of ancient precedent in the Ambrosian and Roman Rites.

At the time of the hymn or anthem *a sermon* may be preached. This is the traditional place for a sermon at the Office, and perhaps the best place if the sermon is *not* related to the readings. *An offering* may also be received and presented at this time. This should be done unobtrusively, and note should be taken that there is no provision for a presentation sentence or hymn.

Authorized intercession and thanksgiving may follow. These may be taken from the Prayers and Thanksgivings on pages 860 and following or elsewhere. If several are used, they ought to be arranged in a logical order, perhaps following the categories of intercession listed with the Prayers of the People on page 383. A rubric on page 142 also provides:

> *In the Intercessions and Thanksgivings, opportunity may be given for the members of the congregation to express intentions or objects of*

prayer and thanksgiving, either at the bidding, or in the course of the
prayer; and opportunity may be given for silent prayer.

Discretion should be used in the selection of prayers, so that their
length is kept within reason. The intercessions and thanksgivings
should be said rather than sung. They may be concluded with *The
General Thanksgiving* (said by all) and *A Prayer of St. Chrysostom.*
All the material in this section is for *optional use.*

Various options are provided for the conclusion of the Office. It may
conclude with *the dismissal* and/or *one of three sentences.* "Alleluia,
alleluia" may be added to the versicle and response of the dismissal
during Easter Season. The dismissal is properly the deacon's function.
Music for the dismissal is found in the Hymnal at S 24–25, S 31–32,
S 54–55, and S 65–66 (the same tone in each case for use at ordinary
times and in Easter Season, printed separately for each of the Offices).
The sentence may be monotoned; music for the first of the sentences,
customarily known as "the Grace," is found at the end of the music for
the Great Litany in the Accompaniment Edition at S 67. It has become
customary to conclude the Office by signing oneself with the cross
during the final sentence. A bishop may conclude the Office with a
blessing instead of this sentence (using the sign of the cross or the
outstretched hand). Tones for blessing are found in *The Altar Book*
and in *Music for Ministers and Congregations.* A rubric also permits
a *sermon* to be preached after the Office, but this seems the least
desirable place for it. Candles are extinguished unobtrusively and
officiants and choir leave in a silent procession. There is no provision
for a hymn at this point, and none is intended.

An Order of Worship
for the Evening

This is basically an ancient form of Evening Prayer, whose ceremonial
actions were the lamplighting and the oblation of incense. It may be
used in a variety of ways:

1. As a festal introduction to Evening Prayer. When used in this way, after the Phos hilaron or other hymn Evening Prayer continues with the psalm(s). This would be an appropriate usage for Evening Prayer on Sundays and greater feasts and their eves and during Easter Season.

2. As the introduction to an evening Eucharist. When used in this way, after the Phos hilaron or other hymn (the Gloria in excelsis may be used) the Eucharist continues with the salutation and collect of the day. The Prayer Book prescribes this usage for the Vigil Eucharist of Pentecost; *The Book of Occasional Services* prescribes it for the Vigil Eucharist of the First Sunday after Epiphany and All Saints' Day or Sunday (all baptismal feasts).

3. As the introduction to another Office or devotion, which follows the Phos hilaron or other hymn. *The Book of Occasional Services* prescribes this usage for evening Services of Lessons and Carols for Advent and Christmas, a Service for New Year's Eve, and a Service for All Hallows' Eve.

4. As the introduction to a meal or other activity. In this case, the Phos hilaron or other hymn is followed by the Lord's Prayer and a grace or blessing or the blessing of foods.

5. As a complete evening Office. In this form it might be used as a Saturday Vigil of the Resurrection, as in the Canadian *Book of Alternative Services*. An outline for such a Resurrection Vigil is provided below.

Preparations

Candles should be in place around the church, ready to be lit after the prayer for light. If there is a choir for this service, it might be best if they were in place before the entrance procession. The church should be dark or partially so. If incense is to be used, the censer should be prepared. During the Easter Season, the Paschal Candle should be lit. In Advent, the wreath should be in place. No musical prelude is appropriate before this service. When the Order is used before a meal, it will take place at a table and the only ceremonial action will be the lighting of the table candles.

In the Catholic tradition, full vestments will be used, while in the Evangelical tradition only the basic vestments (alb or cassock and surplice) will be used. The Catholic preference is for the use of incense, the Evangelical preference for omitting it. The customary musical preferences noted above will be true for this service as well.

This is a new service to the Anglican tradition, and its focal point is the evening oblation of light and incense. For such a festive service, full vestments and a sung rendition of the service seem appropriate. Ceremonial notes for Morning and Evening Prayer also apply for this service, unless otherwise noted.

The Entrance and Lamplighting

The officiants enter the darkened church in a silent procession, preceded by acolyte(s) with candle(s). This part of the service may be led from the center of the chancel before the altar or from the seats. In Easter Season, the acolytes will enter without candles, and this part of the service will be led from the Paschal Candle. *The versicle and response* that open the service are sung or said by the officiant. Music for this is found in the Hymnal at S 56 and S 57. *A short lesson* is chanted or read, without announcement or conclusion. Appropriate general lessons are printed in the text of the service; other lessons appropriate for feasts and seasons are listed on page 108. The short lesson may be omitted when a lesson is to be read later in the service, or when one of the responsories (lucernaria) from *The Book of Occasional Services* follows. Music for the short lesson may be found at S 449 in the Accompaniment Edition of the Hymnal. *The Prayer for Light* is then sung or said. Appropriate Prayers, with seasonal variations, are printed or listed in the text of the service; others may be used. Music for this collect, and for others in the service, may be found in the Accompaniment Edition of the Hymnal at S 447 and S 448; or collects may be monotoned. If candles have been used in the entrance procession, they may now be placed on the altar; if processional torches have been used, they may be placed beside the altar. While the (altar candles and other) candles are being lit from the candles brought in at the entrance or (in Easter Season) from the Paschal Candle, *a psalm or a responsory* may be sung or said. Appropriate psalms are listed on page 143; the lucernaria are found in *The Book of Occasional Services* with directions for their use. Artificial lighting may be turned on at this time as required. Music for these responsories is found in the Accompaniment Edition of the Hymnal at S 305 through S 320. The *Phos hilaron or an Office hymn* follows. During the psalm or responsory the thurifer may cense the church by walking around it while candles are being lit, returning to the center of the chancel to stand before the altar and offer incense during the hymn. Later usage would have the altar (and also, if desired, the people) censed during the Phos hilaron. However, if the altar (and people) are to be censed, the Magnificat or other canticle later in the service is the traditional place to do so.

The Order as an Evening Service

If the order is to be used with another service, the rubrics of that service are now followed. If it is to be used as an evening Office, the entrance and lamplighting are the invitatory of the service.

The Psalter: *The psalm or psalms* follow. They may be taken from the Daily Office Lectionary, the proper of the day, and/or the list given on page 143. Antiphons may be used with the psalms. They may be said or sung together, antiphonally, or responsorially. Sources of music are noted in the section on the Psalter for Morning and Evening Prayer above, along with various modes of rendition. In this service, responsorial recitation is appropriate. After each psalm, *silence* may be kept. Each psalm may be followed with a collect. Appropriate psalter collects are given in the psalters of the Canadian *Book of Alternative Services* and the Minister's Edition of the *Lutheran Book of Worship.* There are also collections of psalter collects from mediaeval sources. For music, see above.

The Lesson(s): *One or more readings* from the Scriptures now follow. Lessons may be taken from the Daily Office Lectionary or the proper of the day; or others suitable to the occasion may be used. Silence may follow the lesson(s). If more than one lesson is used, there may be *a sung response* between lessons (such as a responsory, a canticle, a psalm, or a hymn). *A sermon, homily, or a passage from Christian literature* may follow the readings, as at Morning and Evening Prayer.

The Magnificat or some other canticle or hymn of praise then follows. Incense may now be offered before the altar, or the altar (and people) may now be censed. In this Office the Magnificat is an independent part of the Office, rather than a response to the readings.

The Prayers: *A litany or other suitable devotions* follow. Suffrages B at Evening Prayer (music at S 63 and S 64) or one of the forms for the Prayers of the People, particularly I (music at S 106), III (music at S 107) or V (music at S 108) would be appropriate. *The Lord's Prayer* should be included in the devotions; it might follow the suggested intercessions given above immediately. It may be monotoned or sung to S 119 or S 148. *A collect* proper to the day or season, or one printed in the text of this Office or in the Offices of Evening Prayer or Compline may conclude the Prayers. The deacon properly leads the Intercession; all sing the Lord's Prayer; the officiant recites the collect.

The Conclusion: *An additional hymn* may be sung here. *A procession to an appropriate station* might be made during this hymn, as suggested for Morning and Evening Prayer. The service concludes with *a Blessing and/or a Dismissal. The Peace* may then be exchanged. The dismissal is properly given by the deacon. Music for Blessings is given in *The Altar Book* and *Music for Ministers and Congregations.* Music for Dismissals is found at S 174, S 175, and S 176. Music for the Peace is found at S 111. The candles should be extinguished unobtrusively and the officiants (and choir) leave in a silent procession.

A Saturday Vigil of the Resurrection

In the outline below of this form of the Order of Worship for the
Evening, sources for music are given when not cited above.
Ceremonial directions are given when different from those given
above. The service would not be appropriate on Easter Eve, or when a
Vigil Eucharist is to be celebrated on the eves of the First Sunday after
Epiphany, Pentecost, and All Saints' Sunday, or when a feast replaces
the Sunday propers.

V. and R., page 109

Prayer for Light
seasonal as appropriate
in ordinary time, collect for Saturday, page 134

Responsory (lucernarium)

Phos hilaron or Office Hymn

The Psalm (responsorial rendition)
Psalm 118:1–4, 14–18, 19–24, 25–29, Gloria Patri
Refrain
>   Alleluia   *or*
>   Hymnal S 381 antiphon   *or*
>   Hymnal S 384
Music
>   The Psalm and Alleluia are to be found in the *Gradual Psalms* for
>   Easter Monday (A, B, or C). Verses 1–4 and 19–24 will need to be
>   pointed. If the second or third alternative for the refrain is used, it will
>   need to be transposed up a third.

Collect: third collect for Easter Day (short ending)

The Reading: A Gospel of the Resurrection
All stand and the Gospel is announced and concluded as a Gospel at the
Eucharist. Tones for the Gospel are found in *The Altar Book* and *Music for
Ministers and Congregations.* This Gospel should be read by the officiant

from the pulpit. Incense and torches may appropriately be carried before it. The following are appropriate Gospels for this service: Matthew 28:1–10, 16–20; Mark 16:1–7; Mark 16:9–20; Luke 23:55—24:9; Luke 24:13–25; John 20:1–10; John 20:11–18; John 20:19–31; John 21:1–14. Silence follows the Reading.

A Paschal Canticle
Te Deum, Hymnal S 281–288, S 407   *or*
Cantemus Domino, Hymnal S 208–212

The Prayers
Form I, Prayers of the People, Hymnal S 106 (omit the final petition)
The Lord's Prayer
A Prayer of St. Chrysostom
Suffrages B, Evening Prayer, Hymnal S 63 or S 64
Collect for Saturday, page 123

The Procession to the Font
Bidding to Procession by deacon (see Hymnal S 153)
An appropriate hymn
    (Sunday Hymns) 47–52
    (Baptismal Hymns) 294–296, 298–299
V. All of us who were baptized into Christ:
R. Have clothed ourselves with Christ.
Collect: Various Occasions 7, page 252

The Conclusion
Single or threefold Easter Blessing
Dismissal
Peace

The Orders of Service for Noonday and Compline

These services are ceremonially simple. When held in a church or chapel, the officiant may vest in alb (or cassock and surplice). Altar or pavement candles may be lit. The officiant leads the service from his or her seat, and the short lessons are best read in place (not from a lectern). It is appropriate to stand for the entire service in both of these orders, except for the confession and absolution of Compline (at which one may bow or kneel). The sign of the cross may be made at the opening preces of both services, at the beginning of the Penitential Order which precedes Compline and at the prayer for absolution in this Order, and at the Nunc Dimittis and the prayer for blessing which concludes Compline. Complete musical settings for these services are found in the Accompaniment Edition of the Hymnal at S 296–304 (Noonday) and S 321–327 (Compline). Incense is not used with these Offices.

Notes on the Order of Service for Noonday

This Order encompasses the traditional Offices of terce, sext, and nones. One or more of the psalms printed in the text is used; other suitable selections include Psalms 19 and 67, one or more sections of Psalm 119, and a selection from Psalms 120 through 133. Selections from the lessons, hymns, and collects may be adapted to the time of celebration, as indicated in the following table:

Time	Lesson	Hymn	Collect
Forenoon	first	12, 13 19, or 20	first
Noon	second	16, 17, 18, 21, or 22	second or third
Afternoon	third	14, 15, or 23	fourth

If a meditation follows the lesson, it should be very brief. Free intercessions and thanksgivings may be offered before the dismissal.

Notes on Compline

A brief penitential order precedes the actual Office. One or more of the psalms given, or another psalm, is sung or said, with or without antiphon. One of the lessons printed, or another short lesson follows. Hymns 38 through 46 are appropriate at this service. Only one collect is used; it may be followed by a prayer of intercession and free intercessions and thanksgivings. The antiphon is used before and after the Nunc Dimittis. The service concludes with a dismissal and a prayer for blessing.

The Great Litany

The Great Litany is the classic general intercession in the Prayer Book tradition. It is the only general intercession in the regular Sunday services of the English Prayer Book, for the Prayer for the Whole State of Christ's Church is a prayer for the Church only and not for the world. In the English tradition it has been appointed since 1552 for use after Morning Prayer on Wednesdays and Fridays and also on Sundays (where it leads into the Eucharist and has been known as the "Anglican introit"). More recently, because of its marked penitential nature, it has been considered especially appropriate to the seasons of Lent and Advent and has often been sung in procession on Sundays in those seasons. The present Prayer Book suggests that the Supplication which follows the Litany be used with the Litany (in place of what follows the Lord's Prayer) or at the end of Morning or Evening Prayer "especially in times of war, or of national anxiety, or of disaster" (rubric, page 155).

Historically, a litany would be led by a deacon, except for the collects, which would be led by a bishop or presbyter. In the absence of a deacon, it would be led by a lay person or cantor, an assisting presbyter, or the officiant. Traditionally the officiant has vested in cope for the litany when sung in procession, deacons in dalmatic. Before the Eucharist, the celebrant might better wear a chasuble. Evangelicals will prefer to use the basic vestments only—the alb or cassock and surplice (perhaps with stole when recited before the Eucharist.

The Great Litany was set to music by John Merbecke, whose setting is found in the Hymnal at S 67. Music for the supplication is found in the Accompaniment Edition at S 338 and S 339.

In present usage, the Great Litany is appropriately recited kneeling after the collects at Morning or Evening Prayer on Wednesdays and Fridays and during Lent; for use in the entrance procession of the Eucharist on Sundays of Lent and Advent (where it ends at the Kyries and replaces all that precedes the salutation and collect); and on Rogation Days (when it may be used in an outdoor procession). When used with the Eucharist, any setting of the Kyrie may replace that printed with the Litany, and the Prayers of the People will, and the confession may, be omitted. No entrance hymn is appropriate in this situation. When the Great Litany is recited in procession, incense may be used. Evangelicals will omit the use of incense and may prefer to say rather than sing the Litany and to recite it kneeling rather than in procession.

CHAPTER 3

The Proclamation of the Word of God

The Holy Eucharist has two major parts:

1. The Proclamation of the Word of God;

2. The Celebration of the Holy Communion.

The liturgy for the Proclamation of the Word of God, which is the concern of this chapter, is also known as "The Word of God," "The Ministry of the Word," and "The Liturgy of the Word." This liturgy has three further divisions:

1. The Entrance Rite;

2. The Word of God;

3. The Prayers, Confession, and Peace.

The heart of this liturgy is the reading of the Scriptures, the section titled "The Word of God," which gives this part of the liturgy its name; and the main visual focus of the liturgy is the lectern and/or pulpit from which the Scriptures are read and proclaimed. Section 1 finds its visual focus in the entrance procession and the station made by the celebrant at its conclusion—before or behind the altar, or at the seats in the chancel. Section 3 finds its visual focus in the place from which the Prayers of the People are led.

Participants

The celebrant is a bishop or presbyter, who presides at both the Proclamation of the Word of God and at the second part of the Eucharist, the Celebration of the Holy Communion. In the absence of bishop or presbyter, *a deacon or lay person* may preside at this first part of the Eucharist. *A deacon,* if present, *reads the Gospel, leads the Prayers of the People, and gives the Invitation to the Confession.* In the absence of a deacon, a (bishop or) presbyter reads the Gospel, a lay person or assisting presbyter leads the Prayers of the People, and the celebrant gives the Invitation to the Confession. *Lay persons* come forward from the congregation to *read the lessons before the Gospel. A cantor may lead the Gradual Psalm and the Alleluia Verse or Tract* between the lessons and may also lead the people in the Kyrie, Trisagion, Gloria in excelsis, or other canticle before the collect. *The choir may lead the congregation* in the entry song, in the responses to the chants between the lessons, in the Kyrie, Trisagion, Gloria in excelsis, or other canticle before the collect, in the Creed, and in the responses to the Prayers of the People and other responses. In the absence of a cantor, they may carry out the cantor's functions; they may also at times, sing the entrance song and the song between the lessons in place of the congregation (as "anthems"). Acolytes (crucifer, torchbearers, thurifer) may also assist the celebrant. Detailed notes on eucharistic vestments for participants are to be found in Chapter 1.

Preparations

If the full Eucharist is to be celebrated, preparations for both the Proclamation of the Word of God and the Celebration of the Holy Communion will be made before the service. *The Altar Book,* marked for the service, should be on the altar. Lectionary Texts and/or the Gospel Book or a marked Bible should be in place for the readings.

While the Gospel Book is sometimes placed on the altar, it is perhaps best placed in the pulpit or at the lectern or at the gospeller's seat to avoid visually confusing the focus of the two parts of the Eucharist. Communion vessels (including the proper number of chalices and patens (or other containers for bread) and communion linens (corporal, pall, and purificators), a cruet of water, and (if used) a lavabo dish and towel, as well as the receiving basin for alms, should be on the credence. Chalice and paten may be vested, but this nineteenth-century custom has no real point, and is perhaps best avoided. Alms basins should be ready for the ushers in the nave, and bread and wine for the service should be in suitable containers on the oblations table. Candles at the altar and lectern and any standing torches should be lit unobtrusively before the service. If incense is used, the censer should be prepared.

Ceremonial Notes

Celebrant and assistants take the posture and use the gestures for prayer suggested in Chapter 1, though a celebrant who holds a book to read prayers will of necessity omit the hand gestures (the Roman Catholic custom of having someone hold the book for the celebrant seems unduly fussy). The entire liturgy for this part of the Rite may be led from seating in the chancel. If the seating is beside rather than behind the altar, the celebrant and assistants may move to the center as appropriate in the entrance rite and for the Creed and what follows, standing either before or behind the altar. To lead the Prayers of the People, the deacon or other leader may also go to a central position in the nave just before the chancel step (facing the altar except when addressing the people). This is the traditional place for the litany desk, which could be used for this purpose. The Prayers of the People are the only Prayers (except for the confession) in this Rite for which people might kneel; standing is equally appropriate here, and is to be preferred on Sundays and major feasts and their eves and during the Easter Season (as the Council of Nicea decreed).

The sign of the cross may be made at the opening Acclamation and perhaps at the end of the Creed. At the Gospel, the reader may sign the book with the thumb at the announcement and then all may sign forehead, lips, and heart with the thumb, though this traditional triple sign of the cross seems unduly fussy. A bishop or presbyter may make the sign of the cross over the people or stretch a hand over them at the absolution, and the people may sign themselves as a gesture of absolution received. Evangelicals may wish to omit the sign of the cross in these places or (for the absolution) use the alternative gesture.

When the celebrant turns from the altar to address the people, assistants standing at his or her side turn and face inwards.

If incense is used, it is carried in the entrance procession, and the celebrant may cense the altar (by walking around it, or—if it is not freestanding—by walking to each side of it) at the end of the entrance song or during the Kyrie or other hymn used in its place. In this censing, it is perhaps best simply to swing the censer while walking, without attempt to follow any exact pattern. However, the altar is usually censed again during the Offertory, and this initial censing may appropriately be omitted. The censer is also carried in the Gospel procession, and the reader may cense the book during the announcement (if this is done in the midst of the people, someone must hold the book for the reader in this case). The simpler and more ancient use is simply to carry the censer in the two processions and omit censing of both altar and Gospel book.

The following is the traditional order for the entrance procession. It is adjusted as necessary to the participants in the service. If the choir is not seated in or near the chancel, it should be in place before the entrance; indeed, the choir may do so in any case, entering early in a silent procession.

> Thurifer
> Crucifer
> Torchbearers
> Choir
> Vested Lay Assistants

Assisting Presbyters
Deacons
Concelebrating Presbyters
Celebrant

Variations in the order of procession are possible; the general rule is that the final places in the order are the places of honor and that the celebrant should come last. If the choir enters the church by a different entrance than the officiants, a second set of crosses and torches may lead it in a second procession. At smaller services, celebrant and assistants enter in an orderly way, but without a formal procession.

Music

On occasion, the Eucharist will be celebrated without music. The following portions of the service are normally sung when music is used:

Entrance: hymn, psalm, or anthem

After the Acclamation: Kyrie, Trisagion, Gloria, canticle, or hymn

After the Old Testament: psalm, hymn, or anthem

After the Epistle: psalm, hymn, or anthem

Evangelicals may not wish to sing other portions of the Proclamation of the Word of God. Music is also available for the following:

The Acclamations
(Collect for Purity)
(Summary of the Law)
Decalogue and Responses (Rite I)
Collect
Lessons before the Gospel
The Gospel
The Creed
Prayers of the People and Collect
The Peace

At a solemn celebration in the Catholic tradition, this entire portion of the liturgy would be sung, except for the confession and sermon (and possibly the collect for purity and summary of the law). Contemporary usage hesitates to sing the lessons, in the conviction that reading them more effectively conveys their meaning. There is also a certain hesitation to sing the Prayers of the People, lest the active participation of the people be discouraged. If the Creed is sung, it should be in a setting known to the people, for this as the people's affirmation of faith should not be taken from them.

I. *The Entrance Rite*
The People and Priest Gather in the Lord's Name.

The Prayer Book prints four options for the entrance rite (apart from the special forms of the rite in Proper Liturgies and for other services): the standard rite (printed in the text of the service), the Order of Worship for the Evening, the Great Litany at the Entrance, and the Penitential Order. The original entrance rite in the Western tradition consisted of entrance song (introit psalm), greeting (salutation), and prayer (collect). In the course of history, this rite (whose purpose is to assemble the people in God's name for worship and to constitute them as the Church) has become encumbered with doublets of these elements and other devotional material, so that the whole shape of the liturgy became distorted and lost its proper proportions (the readings were shortened as the entrance grew longer). It would be possible, with Rite II, to restore something of the clean lines of the ancient rite, as follows:

Acclamation (before entry)

Introit (during the entry)

> Kyrie, Gloria, Trisagion, *or* other canticle
>
> *or* psalm
>
> *or* hymn

Greeting and collect (conclusion of entry)

A rubric in the Additional Directions notes that necessary announcements may be made before the service. Announcements at this point would best relate to the service itself and might be made before or after the opening hymn (if there is one). Most of the Proper Liturgies to be considered in the next chapter have in fact simplified the entrance rite.

The Standard Rite

Entrance Song: When music is used, the ministers customarily make their entrance during a *hymn, psalm, or anthem*. For congregational music, it is helpful to have the choir part way into the church before the music begins. If the entrance song is an anthem (that is, sung by the choir rather than the congregation), the choir should be in place, as it should also be if its seating is elsewhere than in or near the chancel. At times, all may enter to instrumental music or in silence. There may be times when the entrance song is sung after all have made their entrance (in which case its purpose is to set the theme for the service rather than to "cover" the entrance). A hymn is probably the entrance song of preference in our tradition. It may be related to the feast, the season, or the propers, or (especially in ordinary time) it may be a general hymn of praise. The traditional introit in Western usage is an antiphonal psalm sung by the choir (an "anthem" in Prayer Book terms). The psalm shrank to a single verse with antiphon and Gloria Patri over the course of time. The seasonal and festal introits elaborate the theme of the feast; those used in ordinary time in the past simply used the psalms in course, and have little to commend them today. A responsorial psalm such as the Venite (used for the introit in the Byzantine tradition) might appropriately be sung at the entrance in our rite. On the whole, however, hymns are the best choice here. The entrance song will, of course, be omitted in services without music. It is also possible in Rite II, as noted above, to sing the Acclamations before the entrance and to make the entrance during the Kyrie, Trisagion, Gloria, other canticle, or hymn.

Acclamation: When the entrance has been made (or before it is made, if the last option above is used), the celebrant begins the Acclamation. Alternative Acclamations are printed for use in Lent and Easter Season. Only one Acclamation is used at a service. The Acclamations may be omitted with Rite I. Music for the Acclamations is found at S 76 through S 83 in the Hymnal.

Devotions: In Rite I, the traditional devotional material from prior Prayer Books is retained. The celebrant says or sings the Collect for Purity, and may say or sing the Ten Commandments or the Summary of the Law. The collect and summary are best monotoned if sung, although the collect tone at S 447 and the tone for short lessons at S 449 might be used. Music for the Ten Commandments is found at S 353. If they are used, the Kyrie of the following section will be omitted. In Rite II the Collect for Purity may be said or sung; it is preferable to omit it. The Summary and Commandments are not part of Rite II.

The Canticle: The Kyrie, Trisagion, and Gloria in excelsis are all entrance music (thus duplicating the entrance song). The Kyrie is the remnant of a Roman entrance litany; the Trisagion, a Byzantine refrain originally used with an entrance psalm; and the Gloria, a morning canticle which once served as a "bridge" between the morning Office and the Eucharist. *The Kyrie (in Greek or English) and the Trisagion* are alternatives in this Rite required in Lent and Advent. They may be used on any day outside of Christmas Season, the Sundays of Easter Season and the days of Easter Week, and Ascension Day. In Rite I they may be used on these days also *together with* the Gloria or other canticle. The Kyrie is more easily said responsively in threefold form (as it is printed); it may be sung threefold, sixfold, or ninefold in a variety of styles. Music for the Kyrie is found in the Hymnal at S 84–89 and S 356–359 (Greek), S 90–93 (English, Rite I), and S 94–98 (English, Rite II). The Trisagion, printed for responsive use, may be repeated three times. Music for it is found at S 99–102 and S 360.

The *Gloria in excelsis or another canticle or hymn of praise* is used throughout Christmas Season, on all Sundays of Easter Season and days of Easter Week, and on Ascension Day. It may be used on other days as desired, except on Sundays and ordinary weekdays of Advent and Lent. It is traditionally used for all major feasts and all days of Easter Season. A chart at S 355 suggests various canticles for use in this place in the rite. Music for the canticles (including the Gloria in excelsis) is found at S 177–288 and S 393–407. A hymn may also be used here. Metrical settings of the canticles would be appropriate and are listed on pages 680–681 of the Accompaniment Edition of the Hymnal. Other hymns might also be used. If a hymn is used here, it would make most sense to omit the entrance song, say or sing the acclamation before the entrance, and use this hymn as the entrance song; or to enter in silence and then begin with the acclamation. It is perhaps to be regretted that it is not possible, as in the Canadian *Book of Alternative Services,* to go directly from the acclamation to the collect in services without music.

The Salutation and Collect: The celebrant turns to the congregation and greets them, then sings or says the collect, returning to the original position. The collect may be said or sung on a monotone or to either of the two tones found at S 447–448 (they are also in *The Altar Book*).

It is preferable for the congregation to stand throughout the entrance rite in this form.

The Order of Worship for the Evening at the Entrance

For an evening Eucharist, this provides a very appropriate entrance rite. After the Phos hilaron or Office hymn, the Eucharist continues with the salutation and collect of the day. The Gloria in excelsis may be used in place of the Phos hilaron; however, since the Gloria is a morning hymn and the Phos hilaron an evening hymn, it is perhaps best to retain the Phos hilaron. For further details, refer to the section on this Order in chapter 2.

The Great Litany at the Entrance

The Litany was used for a processional entrance at an early stage of the Roman Rite (a usage preserved in the Easter Vigil of that Rite). The Kyrie in the standard entrance rite is a remnant of this entrance Litany. In Lent and Advent it is particularly appropriate to use the Litany at the entrance. In this case, the Great Litany ends with the Kyrie (which may be sung to any setting), the Prayers of the People are omitted, and the Confession may be omitted. The entrance procession should take the normal route when the Great Litany is sung, or all may enter silently and the Litany may be sung or said kneeling. No hymn is appropriate before the Litany, and the older custom of entering first, and then circling the church while the Litany is sung does not have much point to it. Processions properly move from one place to another. For further details, see the section on the Great Litany in Chapter 2.

The Penitential Order at the Entrance

This Order is perhaps better used as a separate service. When used to open the Eucharist (as a penitential order does in the present Roman Catholic and Lutheran services) it presents awkward shifts of theme and tone at the beginning of the Eucharist. The rationale is that repentance is an appropriate preparation for worship (as at the Daily Office). However, repentance is perhaps better seen as a response to the Word of God proclaimed and a preparation for the exchange of the Peace. If used with the Eucharist, this Order is most appropriate during Lent (and perhaps Advent).

Entrance Song: as in the standard rite, the entrance may be made during *a hymn, psalm, or anthem* or in silence or during instrumental music. In this case, music should probably be penitential in character. For further details on the entrance song and entrance, see above under the standard rite.

Acclamation: after the entrance, *the Acclamation* is said or sung.

The Exhortation or a homily may follow when this order is used as a separate service (but not when it is used with the Eucharist).

The Decalogue may then be said or sung. The music is found at S 353 and S 354 (Rites I and II). *One of three passages of Scripture* (The Summary of the Law, 1 John 1:8, 9, or Hebrews 4:14, 16) may be read by the celebrant.

The Bidding and Confession follow, with the same forms as in the Eucharist itself. The celebrant rises to give *the absolution* (in the same form as in the Office in each rite), using the sign of the cross or the outstretched hand.

Suitable prayers and the Grace or a blessing may conclude the order when used as a separate service.

The Kyrie, Trisagion, or Gloria follows when the order is used to introduce the Eucharist, and the entrance rite then concludes with the salutation and collect.

2. *The Word of God*

The People and Priest Proclaim and Respond to the Word of God.

The reading of the Scriptures is the heart of the liturgy for the Proclamation of the Word of God. The Principal Service Lectionary provides two lessons, a Psalm, and a Gospel for each proper. The commemorations of *Lesser Feasts and Fasts* provide a Lesson, a Psalm, and a Gospel for each proper. In the Calendar of the Church Year, the Prayer Book provides rules of precedence which tell what to do when two propers fall on the same day. Similar rules are provided in *Lesser Feasts and Fasts* for occasions when a commemoration falls on one of the weekdays of Lent or Easter Season.

The lectern and/or pulpit are the focal point(s) for this section of the Proclamation of the Word of God; those not involved in reading remain at their seats. When the Nicene Creed concludes this section of the rite, the celebrant and assistants (if seated at the side of the chancel) may either remain at their seats or move to the center before the altar and lead it facing the altar (liturgical East).

The first lesson is normally taken from the Old Testament when there are three readings. In Easter Season, however, the Acts of the Apostles is read as the first lesson. When there are only two readings, this lesson may be from either the Old Testament (as on Lenten weekdays) or from the New. Directions for announcing and concluding the lessons are printed in the text of the service. Chapter and verse citations may be given if the people follow the reading in their own Bibles; otherwise they are perhaps best omitted. Unless members of the congregation find it difficult to hear the lessons, it is preferable that they listen to the reader, rather than follow lessons from a printed text. The lesson is read from the lectern, preferably by a lay person who comes forward from the congregation. For small weekday Eucharists, the celebrant may need to read this lesson (as well as the others). This and the second lesson may be monotoned or sung according to the directions found in *The Altar Book* and *Music for Ministers and Congregations.* The congregation is seated for this (and the following) lesson. *A period of silence* should follow the lesson.

A psalm, hymn, or anthem: The rubrics allow for an extensive variety of musical responses to this and the following lesson. However, the psalm printed in the lectionary is the normative response, and should be recited even in services without music. The psalm is traditionally recited as a responsory, led by a cantor, who may stand at the lectern, the pulpit, or beside either, or remain in the choir stalls. Plainsong settings of all the gradual psalms (as well as Alleluia Verses and Tracts, which follow the next reading or—when there is only one reading— follow the gradual psalm) are available under the title *Gradual Psalms* in five volumes from the Church Hymnal Corporation. Responsorial settings in Sarum plainsong are also available in James Barrett's *Psalmnary,* and Gelineau settings are available as well. *The Ionian Psalter,* by Peter R. Hallock, published by Ionian Arts, is a responsorial setting of the psalms in an Anglican Chant style (the verses are through-composed for singing by the choir), with a congregational refrain. The psalms, with or without refrains, may also be sung by all together or antiphonally to plainsong tones, or to Anglican or Simplified Anglican Chant tunes or tunes from the

Lutheran Book of Worship (see notes on the psalms in the chapter on the Daily Office above). The Gloria Patri is traditionally omitted with gradual psalms. A metrical psalm may also be sung in this place. A list of psalms with metrical settings in the Hymnal is found on page 679 of the Service Music volume of the Accompaniment Edition of the Hymnal. *A New Metrical Psalter* (Church Hymnal Corporation) is a collection of metrical texts in common hymn meters for all gradual psalms. On occasion, an anthem setting of the psalm text, if available, might be sung by the choir in this place; or another appropriate hymn or anthem may be sung. The congregation would remain seated for a psalm or anthem; it should rise if a hymn (or metrical psalm) is to be sung.

The second lesson (if appointed) is taken from the New Testament. It is read from the lectern in the same way as the first and may be sung in the same way. The congregation is seated for this lesson. *A period of silence* should follow.

A psalm, hymn, or anthem: the rubrical provision for the musical response to the second lesson is the same as that for the first. In this case, however, no provision is made in the Lectionary. The traditional response (except in Lent) is the responsorial rendition of a verse of Scripture with "Alleluia" as the refrain. In Lent, the cantor (or choir) traditionally replaced this with a section of psalmody sung without refrain (the tract). Alternatively, a single verse of Scripture may be sung with no refrain. Plainsong provision for these verses and tracts is found in *Gradual Psalms,* as noted above. The cantor might sing the verse or tract at or beside the lectern or pulpit or from the choir stalls. A hymn, known as the sequence, is also traditional in this place. A hymn used here should be related to the preceding lesson or to the Gospel or (at times) to the general theme of the feast or season. Both sequence and verse or tract may be sung; if this is done, perhaps the verse (or tract) should immediately precede the Gospel, to which it is normally closely related. Another option here is the use of a canticle, seasonally or thematically chosen. Since the Daily Office is less frequently sung on Sundays than it once was, this choice is one way of preserving the heritage of canticles in Anglican worship. An anthem related to the lesson or Gospel is also appropriate. The congregation would normally remain seated for an anthem, but rise for a verse, tract, canticle, or hymn.

The Gospel: the Gospel is read from the lectern, the pulpit, or the midst of the congregation. A pulpit is in origin the Gospel lectern and should be used as such. However, if the preacher is not the gospeller, it may prove convenient for the preacher to go to the pulpit during the musical response to the lesson before the Gospel while the gospeller goes to the lectern. If there is no pulpit, the lectern should be used for the Gospel. It has also become customary in recent years to read the Gospel from the midst of the congregation. It may prove difficult to see or hear the gospeller in this place, however. The deacon, when present, reads the Gospel. If no deacon is present, it is perhaps best for the preacher (if ordained) to read the Gospel. All stand for the reading of the Gospel. Directions for announcing and concluding the Gospel are found in the text of the rite. Directions for singing the Gospel may be found in *The Altar Book* or *Music for Ministers and Congregation*. Because this is the climactic reading of the Proclamation of the Word of God, it is appropriate to have the gospeller accompanied by torchbearers and, if desired, to carry incense in the procession. The Gospel book may be censed when the Gospel is announced. The cross should not be carried in this procession; it distracts attention from the Gospel book, which should provide the visual focus here. At the announcement and conclusion of the Gospel, the gospeller raises the book before the congregation (*not* toward the altar) for their acclamation. After the Gospel, the gospeller (and acolytes) return unobtrusively to their seats; or the gospeller remains to preach the sermon, while the acolytes return. *No hymn* is provided for by rubrics between Gospel and sermon and none should be sung. The lingering custom of "sandwiching" the gospel between stanzas of a hymn should be discontinued. A rubric on page 406 provides:

> *When a portion of the congregation is composed of persons whose native tongue is other than English, a reader appointed by the celebrant may read the Gospel in the language of the people, either in place of, or in addition to, the Gospel in English.*

The Sermon: the purpose of the sermon is to relate the lessons, and particularly the Gospel, to the situation of the congregation—to break open their meaning for us today. A sermon should always be preached on Sundays and major feasts; at least a brief comment on the lessons should be offered at other times. On a saint's day, the biography from *Lesser Feasts and Fasts* might be read here.

The Nicene Creed is required on Sundays and major feasts; it may be omitted at other times. It is part of the congregation's response in faith to the Scriptures. The celebrant would ordinarily lead it, though the preacher might also do this. If seated at the side, the celebrant (and assistants) may wish to go to the center of the chancel and face the altar (liturgical East) for the Creed. It may be said or sung; if sung, it may be intoned by the celebrant or begun by all in unison. It may be monotoned or sung to S 103 (traditional text) or S 104 or S 361 (ICET text). It should be sung only if the congregation can sing it; it is a congregational text and the people should be able to join in its recitation. It has been customary to conclude it with the sign of the cross. It has also been customary to bow during the "incarnate" clause (or until the resurrection clause). A genuflection here, once common among Roman Catholics, is no longer usual. In fact, both bow and genuflection might better be omitted as distracting. The sign of the cross too might be omitted.

On baptismal feasts, the Nicene Creed should be replaced by the Renewal of Baptismal Vows at all celebrations of the Eucharist, even if there are no baptisms. It would not be appropriate to attempt to sing this.

A rubric on page 407 notes, "Necessary announcements may be made …after the Creed…" Announcements at this place would properly be those related to petitions offered in the Prayers of the People which follow.

3. The Prayers, Confession, and Peace

The People and Priest Pray
for the Church and the World and Exchange the Peace

The Prayers of the People may be seen as part of our response to the Word of God read and proclaimed. Leading these prayers is the deacon's function; summing them up in the concluding collect is the function of the bishop or presbyter as celebrant. The Peace is a sign of the reconciliation established by Jesus between God and God's people: as a gesture it now more commonly takes the form of a handclasp or embrace than of the original kiss. The Peace acts as a link or bridge between the Proclamation of the Word of God and the Celebration of the Holy Communion. The confession is an appropriate preparation for the exchange of the Peace. When it is omitted, a penitential petition should be included in the Prayers of the People. The position for the leader and the posture for prayer have been noted earlier in this chapter. The celebrant will preside from the same place used at the entrance rite.

The Prayers of the People: Except under special circumstances, as in the Pastoral Offices, these prayers include intercessions for the following (rubric, page 383):

> *The Universal Church, its members and its mission*
> *The Nation and all in authority*
> *The welfare of the world*
> *The concerns of the local community*
> *Those who suffer and those in any trouble*
> *The departed (with commemoration of a saint when appropriate)*

The traditional Prayer Book form is printed with Rite I. In the first paragraph it would be best to use "all people" for "all men" to avoid gender-specific language. The rubrics give scope for this. This form has the disadvantage of being basically a monologue: a response may now be used after each paragraph, but this usage is awkward. Six forms are printed on pages 383–393 for use as Prayers of the People.

Forms I and V are litanies (based on Byzantine models); Form II is a series of biddings with silence; Form IV, a series of short prayers, each followed by silence and a common versicle and response; Form III, a short series of suffrages; Form VI a series of biddings said responsively with several suffrages and a confession which may be used. Each may be adapted in some way for particular petitions or biddings. A series of collects (as on Good Friday) or any form of intercession which conforms to the outline above may also be used. Forms I and V are probably most suitable for the Sunday Eucharist; Forms II and IV might be used on Sundays or weekdays; and the briefer Form III is appropriate for a weekday Eucharist.

Except for the form printed in Rite I, all the printed intercessions conclude with a collect recited by the celebrant. The doxology printed for Form V is best avoided: historically it is the publicly recited conclusion to a silently recited prayer. If the confession of Form VI is used, an absolution may replace the collect. Forms I–VI may be introduced by the celebrant with a sentence of invitation related to the occasion, the season, or the propers.

Holy Baptism, Confirmation, the Marriage Service, the Burial Office, Episcopal Services (except for the Consecration of a Church), Ash Wednesday, Good Friday, and Thanksgiving Day all have special forms of the Prayers of the People, although the regular forms may be used in addition at Baptism and Confirmation. A special version of Form V is found in *The Book of Occasional Services* for Sundays when candidates for Baptism are enrolled (traditionally the first Sundays in Lent and Advent); this book also has a special litany for healing services. The Great Litany when used at the entrance with the Eucharist is also a form of the Prayers of the People.

Directions for singing the form printed in the text of the Rite I Eucharist may be found in *The Altar Book*. Musical settings for Forms I–VI are found in the Hymnal at S 106, S 362, S 107, S 108, S 109, and S 363 respectively. *The Altar Book* has directions for singing the solemn biddings and collects of Good Friday. Music for the proper Prayers of the People for Episcopal Services (the Litany for

Ordinations), the anniversary of the dedication of a church (a Litany of Thanksgiving for a Church), and Thanksgiving Day are found at S 390–392. Music for the baptismal litany (for Baptism and Confirmation) is found in *The Altar Book* and at S 75. Directions for singing the concluding collects is found with the music for the individual forms. It has long been customary in Anglican tradition to sing litanies and suffrages. Of these forms, I, III, and V lend themselves best to singing. If singing hinders the active participation of people in the prayers, however, they are better said.

Parochial intercessions may be included in the petitions or biddings of Forms I (petitions), II (biddings), III (final bidding), IV (petitions), V (petitions), and VI (biddings). A mimeographed form with blanks to fill in facilitates the inclusion of these intercessions by the deacon or other person leading the Prayers of the People.

In Forms I, IV, and V, the celebrant (or leader of the intercessions) may invite the particular petitions of the congregation before the intercession begins, or they may be offered in the silence before the collect. Forms II, III, and VI indicate where the petitions of the congregation may be added.

Any suitable collect may be used to conclude the Prayers of the People. A lesser feast may be commemorated by using its proper collect here. A prayer for mission from Morning or Evening Prayer, a collect from these Offices (if suitable to the time and day), a seasonal collect, a collect from Various Occasions, or one of the Prayers and Thanksgivings on pages 810–841 may be used. The Morehouse-Barlow Lectionary Calendar lists suggestions for specific days. Collects here may be concluded with the short ending (without doxology).

In Form II, which is a series of biddings, the leader should face the people. In the Rite I form and Forms I, IV, and V, the leader may face the people for the initial bidding, and then turn toward the altar.

If the service is not to continue with the Celebration of the Holy Communion, it now concludes. The rubric on page 407 provides:

A hymn or anthem may then be sung, and the offerings of the people received. The service may then conclude with the Lord's Prayer; and with either the Grace or a blessing, or with the exchange of the Peace.

The Confession: The confession follows, unless the service has begun with the penitential order. It may, however, be omitted on occasion. The rubrics for Baptism, Confirmation, Marriage, and Burial of the Dead make no provision for a confession. Ash Wednesday has a special form of confession—the litany of penitence. The confession may be omitted on Palm Sunday. When the Great Litany has been sung at the entrance, it would be appropriate to omit it also. It might also be omitted in Easter Season. When it is omitted, it would be appropriate to use the penitential petitions of Form I and V and of the Prayers of the People. Form VI has the confession in its text.

The *invitation to confession* is given by the deacon or (in the absence of a deacon) by the celebrant. The long exhortation on page 316 may be used for the invitation. It would be appropriate for the first Sunday of Advent and Lent. In Rite II the confession may be introduced by a sentence of scripture from page 351. An appropriate period of *silence* follows the invitation.

In Rite I, all are directed to kneel for *the confession.* It would also be appropriate to kneel for the confession in Rite II. After the confession, the celebrant rises for *the absolution,* making the sign of the cross or stretching out a hand over the people. In Rite I, one or more of *the comfortable words* may be said by a minister (perhaps the deacon or an assisting presbyter). In Rite I, it is best to avoid the first form of confession and the last two comfortable words because of their gender-specific language.

The Peace: It is appropriate that we should be at peace with one another before we approach the Lord's table. The Peace is first exchanged as a greeting between the celebrant and the congregation. Music for this exchange is found in the Hymnal at S 110 and S 111 (Rites I and II). The Peace may then be exchanged between members of the congregation with any appropriate words and gestures of greeting. The celebrant may go into the congregation to exchange the

Peace, if desired. The Peace may also be exchanged in its Roman Catholic (and 1549) position, before Communion. The position printed in the text is both preferable and more ancient, however.

Morning and Evening Prayer as the Liturgy of the Word

Readings and Psalm: *The Book of Common Prayer* 1979 makes provision for use of Morning or Evening Prayer as the Liturgy of the Word at the Eucharist. On a Sunday or major feast, the readings and psalm will be those of the Principal Service (not the Daily Office) Lectionary. On other occasions (such as a daily service) the propers might be taken from either. The Gospel must be used, and may be announced and concluded as at the Eucharist, the people standing.

The Order of Service: Rubrics provide that the Nicene Creed may replace the Apostles' Creed, that the Lord's Prayer and Suffrages may be omitted, and that intercessions shall conform to the requirements for the Prayers of the People. The service continues at the Eucharist with the Peace. The outline of the Proclamation of the Word of God in this case would be:

(Penitential Order from the Office)
    Sentence
    Invitation, Confession, and Absolution

The Invitatory and the Psalter
    Preces
    Invitatory Psalm, Easter Canticle, Phos hilaron, or hymn
    Psalm(s)

The Lessons
    First lesson
    Canticle
    Second lesson
    Canticle

Gospel
Sermon
Apostles' or Nicene Creed (when appointed)

The Prayers
Salutation and Collect of the Day
Prayers of the People (as at the Eucharist)
Peace

If only two lessons are used, the Gospel would be the second lesson, followed by the canticle and sermon. The flow of the service might be improved if one concluded the Prayers of the People with the Collect of the Day rather than reciting it first. No provision is made for a hymn at the entrance. One might possibly be used on the analogy of the entrance at the Eucharist, though this is probably not intended. Further details on the Office are found in chapter 2.

Vestments: the same vestments should be worn throughout the service: alb (or cassock and surplice) with or without stole, or eucharistic vestments. Changing vestments at the Offertory does not make a point of any significance.

The Proper Liturgies 79

Other Proper Liturgies 101

Other Seasonal Services 106

CHAPTER 4

Proper Liturgies for Special Days

We departed from the order of materials in *The Book of Common Prayer* to consider the liturgy for the Proclamation of the Word of God before the Proper Liturgies for Special Days and Holy Baptism because these two latter sections provide proper liturgies of the Word adapted to particular occasions and it seemed best to turn our attention to the standard forms of that liturgy first.

The Proper Liturgies

Having considered those standard forms, we turn now to the Proper Liturgies for Special Days, which provide services for Ash Wednesday, Palm Sunday, Maundy Thursday, Good Friday, Holy Saturday, and the Great Vigil of Easter. We will then consider other proper liturgies—the baptismal vigils of Pentecost (from *The Book of Common Prayer*) and for the first Sunday after Epiphany or the Baptism of Christ and All Saints' Day or Sunday (from *The Book of Occasional Services*), as well as provisions in *The Book of Occasional*

Services for a Candlemas Procession (before the Eucharist on the Feast of the Presentation), a Rogation Procession, and the Admission of Catechumens (at a Sunday Eucharist) and the Enrollment of Candidates for Baptism (ordinarily on the first Sundays in Lent and Advent). These might be considered optional supplements to the regular services of the Church. Finally, we will note briefly other seasonal services found in *The Book of Occasional Services* which might be considered supplementary optional devotions. These are not proper liturgies which are a part of the regular services of the Church, but popular devotions which have come to be associated with certain seasons and feasts.

Lent, Holy Week, and Easter are the seasons of the Church Year that focus on the very heart of the Christian Gospel—the Cross, the Resurrection, and the gift of the Spirit. The rites for these days are the most ancient seasonal liturgies of the Church. At the Reformation, Archbishop Cranmer radically pruned these ancient rites of the special features which they had developed over the course of the centuries, leaving only the lectionary propers as a means for observing these days and seasons. Yet these seasons are so rich in meaning that later centuries found the Prayer Book provisions very austere indeed, and supplements to the liturgies of Ash Wednesday, Palm Sunday, Maundy Thursday, Good Friday, and Easter Eve (drawn from ancient materials or from more recent Roman Catholic observances) have been widely used. Indeed, many of these services eventually found authorized form in the Episcopal Church in the edition of *Occasional Offices* issued by the Standing Liturgical Commission in 1960. In 1979 similar provisions were incorporated into *The Book of Common Prayer* itself. While the proper liturgies derive from the Catholic tradition, they have an evangelical thrust that would commend them in great measure to the church at large (with the possible exception of the use of ashes—an optional feature of the Ash Wednesday liturgy—and the custom of receiving communion from the Reserved Sacrament—an optional provision of the Good Friday liturgy). In fact, many of these special liturgies are now widely used in other churches of the Reformation—even the customarily non-liturgical ones.

The Pascha, the feast of Christ's Passover from death to Risen life by the way of the cross, is the most ancient of the church's annual feasts. In the first Christian centuries Lent as a preparatory season of forty days (based on the precedent of Christ's post-baptismal fast) and a fifty-day celebratory season extending from Easter to Pentecost (based on the Jewish festival season extending over the same period) developed in relation to the Paschal feast. As baptism and the reconciliation of penitents became associated with the Pascha or Easter, they came to have an increasingly strong impact on the liturgical provisions for Lent, Holy Week, and the Easter season. All of the rites sought to work out and to make real and vivid the full meaning of the Cross and Resurrection of Christ in the life of believers. For this reason, the careful, thoughtful, well-prepared celebration of the Proper Liturgies should be a matter of priority in the life of a parish. The ordinary weekdays of the Lenten and Easter seasons are also important enough that the book of *Lesser Feasts and Fasts* provides propers for a daily Eucharist—with an Old Testament reading, psalm, and Gospel for the weekdays of Lent (apart from Ash Wednesday and Holy Week, for which the Prayer Book makes provision) and a reading from Acts, psalm, and Gospel for the weekdays of Easter Season (apart from Easter Week and Ascension Day, for which the Prayer Book makes provision).

Ash Wednesday and the Lenten Season

Preparation

The Lenten Season has come to have an austere quality to it that seems appropriate to its character as a time of fast and preparation. A feast is best appreciated after a fast. In actual fact, many of the apparently austere characteristics of the season simply preserve features of early Christian worship before it was elaborated in later centuries. Still, the mood is appropriate.

It has become customary to avoid ornament in church during this season. The Lenten array, traditionally unbleached linen trimmed in red and black, covers altar and ornaments in the church, and matching vestments and hangings may be used. It became customary to veil even crosses during Lent because they were thought of as signs of victory. This is certainly appropriate for a Christus Rex or an elaborate jewelled cross. It makes no sense for a crucifix or a simple cross. It is probably more appropriate to substitute a simpler cross than to veil a cross. The later custom of using purple as a penitential color is an alternative to the Lenten array. Flowers are customarily omitted for this season. The mood created should be subdued and serious.

In the Lenten liturgy, signs of festivity are customarily omitted. Alleluia (or Hallelujah) is omitted wherever it normally occurs in a service. The Gloria in excelsis is not used in the entrance rite for the Eucharist. In the office, the Te Deum is not used as an office canticle. In place of the customary blessing, *The Book of Occasional Services* provides *Prayers over the People* as Lenten blessings. In actual fact, this form of blessing is more ancient than the more recent trinitarian form now commonly used.

If ashes are to be used in the Proper Liturgy for Ash Wednesday, these will need to be prepared ahead of time. They are usually made by burning palms from the previous year and preparing ashes from them. Or they may be purchased from suppliers. It should be noted that they are an optional, not mandatory, provision in the liturgy. Those who pay heed to the Gospel for the day may wish to omit their use, or provide basins and towels for worshipers to remove them after the service.

The Entrance Rite

On Ash Wednesday, the Proper Liturgy begins with a radically simplified entrance rite. The officiants enter in silence, or during an appropriate penitential hymn or psalm, and the celebrant begins at once with *the Salutation and Collect of the Day.*

The Ministry of the Word

As usual, *an appropriate reading from the Old Testament, a psalm, an Epistle, and a Gospel* are provided for the ministry of the word. Music for the psalm is found in the *Gradual Psalms,* or other forms of rendition may be used, as customary. Before the Gospel, a seasonal hymn or canticle (such as Canticle 10 or Canticle 14) would be appropriate. *Gradual Psalms* provides a verse or tract for use if desired. The sermon follows; the Creed is omitted.

The Penitential Liturgy

After the sermon, *an exhortation to a holy Lent* is read by the celebrant or minister appointed. The exhortation, drawn from the Canadian Prayer Book, sets the themes of Lent:

> preparation for Holy Week and Easter;
>
> preparation of candidates for baptism;
>
> preparation of the faithful through repentance.

It also sets out the disciplines of the Christian life through which this preparation has traditionally been made.

After the exhortation, *silence* is kept, all kneeling. If desired, *ashes may be imposed.* This rite was first used for those who were admitted to public penance on this day (to receive reconciliation on Maundy Thursday). Later, it was extended to all the faithful. The celebrant first says a *prayer over the ashes,* which designates them as signs of human mortality and penitence. It will probably prove most convenient for the people to come forward to receive ashes in the same place and same manner as for communion. The ashes are customarily put on the forehead in the sign of the cross. A *sentence* is provided for use during the imposition. Note that this is an *optional feature* of the liturgy for the day.

Psalm 51:1–18 is then said or sung kneeling. The psalm may in fact be begun during the imposition. While neither the Hymnal, *Music for Ministers and Congregation,* nor the *Gradual Psalms* provides music for this, a partial setting of Psalm 51 is found in *Gradual Psalms* as the proper psalm for the first Sunday in Lent, Year A, and this might be used if the remainder of the verses were pointed. The psalm might also be sung from *The Anglican Chant Psalter,* or to a plainsong tone, Anglican Chant or Simplified Anglican Chant tune from the Hymnal, or to a tone from the *Lutheran Book of Worship.*

A *litany of penitence* replaces both the confession and the Prayers of the People on this day. It is led by the celebrant (*not* the deacon) on this day. At its conclusion, the celebrant (if bishop or presbyter) rises to pronounce *the absolution* with the customary gesture. If a deacon or lay person leads the service, the prayer for forgiveness appointed for Morning Prayer is used and the officiant remains kneeling. The Peace is then exchanged, and the service continues with the Celebration of the Holy Communion. Rubrics provide:

> In the absence of a bishop or priest [= presbyter], all that precedes may be led by a deacon or lay person.

> The Litany of Penitence may be used at other times and may be preceded by an appropriate invitation and penitential psalm.

The Sunday of the Passion: Palm Sunday

Preparation

The Sunday of the Passion begins Holy Week, the last week of Lent, which has its own character. Beginning with this day, the church follows in liturgical commemoration the last week of Jesus' life. Propers for the Proclamation of the Word of God are provided in the lectionary for each day, and Passion Sunday, Maundy Thursday, Good Friday, and Holy Saturday each have their special forms of liturgical observance. The liturgical color for this week is Passiontide red—a dull oxblood red trimmed with black. If possible, vestments and hangings of this color, rather than ordinary red should be used; certainly red vestments with inappropriate symbols should be avoided. If such hangings and vestments are not available, the Lenten array or

Lenten purple may continue in use until Easter Eve. Musical resources which are especially useful in Holy Week in addition to the usual books are the settings for the services available from Mason Martens, 175 West 72nd Street, New York, New York 10023, and James Barrett's *Psalmnary,* noted in the previous chapter as a source for settings of the gradual psalms. Mason Martens' publications are particularly useful as a source for settings of the Passion. *The Psalmnary* is useful as a source of settings for responsorial psalmody. Whenever *Gradual Psalms* is listed as a resource for such psalms, an alternative setting may be found in the *Psalmnary.* The Appendix gives notes on accompanying such psalmody, and the use of handbells would be particularly effective in services for this week.

For Palm Sunday, palms for the people and for altar decoration will need to be ordered in advance. In earlier ages, branches from local trees and shrubs were used in places where palms were not native. Before the liturgy begins, a place for the liturgy of the palms will need to be prepared: this should be a place apart from the church to which the procession will go—perhaps a place outside or the parish hall. At the very least the procession should start from the narthex or back of the church, not from the altar itself. Palms will be placed on a table for later distribution, or they may be distributed to the people before the liturgy begins. Since the people cannot conveniently carry Prayer Books and Hymnals, the necessary parts and hymns should be printed on a service sheet.

The Liturgy of the Palms

This liturgy replaces the ordinary entrance rite for the principal Eucharist of the day. It commemorates Jesus' triumphal entry into Jerusalem on this day. If possible, as noted above, people gather "at a place apart from the church." *The opening anthem* may be sung by the choir, or may be sung or said as a versicle and response (music at Hymn 153). The celebrant then sings (to one of the usual tones) or says *the opening collect.* The *Gospel account of the entry* designated for the year is then read or sung by a deacon or some other person. It may be treated as a Gospel at the Eucharist (as in *The Altar Book*) or as an ordinary lesson.

The celebrant then sings or says *the Blessing of the Palms* (in the orans position, if the hands are free). At the words, "Let these branches...", it would be appropriate to make the sign of the cross or extend a hand. Music for this blessing is found in *The Altar Book*; music for the responses is found in the Hymnal at Hymn 153. *The palms are then distributed* to all, if this has not been done before the liturgy. *The text which follows* may be sung by the choir as an anthem, or sung or said as a versicle and response. The deacon or other person then gives the *bidding for the procession*. Music for this bidding and for the preceding anthem is also found at Hymn 153. *The procession forms and moves to the church to appropriate hymns, psalms, and anthems.* The traditional psalm is Psalm 118:19–29 and a setting of this for the procession is found at Hymn 157. "All glory, laud, and honor" (Hymn 154 or 155) is the ancient hymn for this procession; "Ride on, ride on in majesty" (Hymn 156) is also appropriate. *A station* may be made during the procession (perhaps at the church door). *A collect* is provided for this. The procession continues into the church and concludes with *the Collect of the Day,* sung or said with the salutation in the chancel.

If it is not possible to gather outside the church or in the narthex, at least choir and children should enter in the procession with the ministers, and the rite may begin at the rear of the church. At services other than the principal celebration, all or part of this liturgy may be used, as suitable. At the least, the Liturgy of the Palms through the blessing and distribution might be used, even if there is no procession.

The Liturgy of the Passion (Ministry of the Word)

The service continues with the Ministry of the Word. At this point, the dominant theme of the service shifts from the triumphal entry to the Passion. In the Western tradition, the Passion is the dominant theme of the liturgy on this day, which anticipates the liturgy of Good Friday, as indeed the first name given to the day in the title indicates.

An *Old Testament reading, psalm, Epistle, and Gospel* are provided for the ministry of the word. *Gradual Psalms* provides a setting for the psalm and for a verse or tract before the Gospel. If a hymn is used before the Gospel, one of the Passion hymns is the appropriate choice. The proper Gospel for this Sunday is *the Passion* for the appropriate year. It is announced as "the Passion" rather than in the customary way, and no response is made either to the announcement or at the conclusion. It may be read or sung in parts, as a dramatic narrative. The readers need not be ordained. The people may be seated until the point indicated in the rubric because of the length of the reading. If the Passion is to be read or sung in parts, all but the narrator may read from their seats (acoustics permitting). All will need copies of the text marked for parts (and music, if the Passion is sung). Music for the Passions is available from Mason Martens. A moment of silence is customarily kept when the narrator reaches the moment of Jesus' death. In cases of necessity, a shorter form of the Passion may be used.

The Eucharist continues, after the Passion and Sermon, with the Prayers of the People, the Peace, and the Celebration of the Holy Communion in accordance with the rubric:

> *When the Liturgy of the Palms has preceded, the Nicene Creed and the Confession of Sin may be omitted at this service.*

In the absence of a bishop or presbyter, a deacon or lay person may lead the liturgy through the prayers of the people.

Maundy Thursday

Preparation

This day, which commemorates the last supper, footwashing, and betrayal, traditionally is observed with an evening Eucharist. Sometimes the Eucharist has been observed in a festive manner (in thanksgiving for the Holy Eucharist); at other times in a subdued manner as appropriate to the eve of the Passion. A festive celebration will use white hangings and vestments and include the Gloria in excelsis; a Passiontide celebration will keep the Passiontide or Lenten array or purple hangings and vestments and omit the Gloria in excelsis. The latter alternative would be preferable, but either is possible.

If the footwashing is to be observed, a place must be prepared for those who participate to sit (where they will be visible to the rest of the congregation). A bowl, a pitcher of water, a sponge, and a towel should be nearby. If communion is to be administered from the Reserved Sacrament on Good Friday, adequate bread and wine should be available on Maundy Thursday to consecrate for this purpose. If it is to be reserved somewhere other than in the usual place, this too will need to be prepared. This should not, however, be an "altar of repose" like that of the unreformed Roman Rite; reservation in this manner is wholly inappropriate to the nature of the day and to Anglican Eucharistic theology.

The Ministry of the Word

The entrance is made in the ordinary way. If the Eucharist is celebrated in a festive manner, the Gloria in excelsis may be sung; it would seem preferable to omit it in keeping with the nature of the occasion as the eve of the Passion, however. A full provision is made for *Old Testament reading, psalm, Epistle, and Gospel. Gradual Psalms* provides a setting of the psalm and a tract and verse. The Johannine Gospel is the preferable alternative (since the Lucan Gospel essentially duplicates the account of the supper in the Epistle) and will in any case be used if the footwashing is to be observed. Eucharistic and Passiontide hymns are appropriate; Hymn 329 or 331 would make an especially appropriate entrance hymn. Eucharistic hymns, when used, should focus on the rite as a memorial of the cross and passion rather than as a means of the Risen Christ's presence.

The Liturgy of the Footwashing (the Maundy)

The special feature of the Eucharist on this evening is *the footwashing,* commemorating Jesus' act of humble service. This follows the sermon (the Creed being customarily omitted). *The Book of Occasional Services* provides an address which may be used, following the sermon, to introduce this special rite. If this ceremony is observed, the celebrant takes off the chasuble and representatives of the congregation come forward to the seats prepared for them and remove shoes and socks or stockings. Then, taking a basin, a pitcher of water, a sponge or cloth, and a towel, the celebrant washes the feet of those who have come forward, assisted by other ministers or acolytes.

The Prayer Book provides several of *the traditional anthems* for this ceremony, which may be sung or said while this is going on. Music for these anthems is found in the appendix to the Accompaniment Edition of the Hymnal at S 344–347. *The hymn "Ubi caritas"* is also traditional for this ceremony. Various translations are found in Hymns 576, 577, 581, and 606. Hymn 602 would also be appropriate here. Other settings of these texts are found in the music for Holy Week published by Mason Martens.

The service continues with the Prayers of the People (for which Collect 6 on page 395 would be especially appropriate), the Confession, the Peace, and the Celebration of the Holy Communion. Eucharistic Prayer D might be especially appropriate for this service. If the sacrament is to be reserved for Good Friday communions, at the time of ablutions the deacon, an assisting presbyter, or the celebrant will place the bread and wine reverently but unobtrusively in the aumbry or other place of reservation. This should be done without ceremony or fuss; the sacramental procession of the unreformed Roman Rite is inappropriate here.

The Book of Occasional Services provides two further rubrics with regard to this service:

> *When the Sacrament is to be reserved for administration on Good Friday, it should be kept in a separate chapel or other place apart from the main sanctuary of the church, in order that on Good Friday, the attention of the congregation may be on the bare main altar.*

If the custom of stripping the Altar is observed as a public ceremony, it takes place after the Maundy Thursday liturgy. It may be done in silence, or it may be accompanied by the recitation of Psalm 22, which is said without Gloria Patri. The following antiphon may be said before and after the Psalm: They divide my garments among them; they cast lots for my clothing.

The author would not recommend either practice in the form suggested in these rubrics. The ordinary aumbry of the church is normally adequate for reservation for Good Friday: devotions before the sacrament reserved should perhaps be discouraged in any case as inconsistent with Anglican theology. In churches where such devotion is customary, however, the rubric makes sense. On this occasion, the focus of devotion should be the cross, not the eucharistic presence. Stripping the altar after the service is in origin a purely practical action (once customary after all services). It may be desirable to do this in preparation for the Good Friday liturgy. However, to use Psalm 22 is to suggest a symbolic relation between this and the stripping of Christ at his crucifixion. This kind of arbitrary and artificial symbolism had a pernicious effect on liturgy in the Middle Ages and should be avoided.

A watch may be kept after the service. It should be kept before the cross, not before the reserved sacrament. While the watch is customarily informal and kept in silence, texts for meditation and appropriate prayers might be provided for use when desired by those keeping the watch.

As *The Book of Occasional Services* notes, a seder is not an appropriate observance on this day. The book does, however, provide special blessings for food and drink at a simple meal or agape on that day. The true Christian Passover Seder is the Eucharist of the Great Vigil of Easter; attempts to mix the Jewish observance with the Christian Eucharist are improper. If desired, a seder following the Jewish ritual might be observed earlier in Lent; while a commentary on this rite might well note it as the precursor to the Christian Eucharist, the seder should not be observed as a Eucharist or joined to a Eucharist.

Good Friday

The core of the Good Friday Liturgy is the Proclamation of the Word of God with its reading of the Passion according to John and its ancient form of the Prayers of the People. To this two other elements have been added:

1. the Adoration of the Crucified;

2. Communion from the Reserved Sacrament.

The adoration of the crucified (or veneration of the cross) dates from the fourth century and Helena's supposed discovery of the true cross. Devotions before the cross are certainly appropriate on this day. Christian practice in regard to Good Friday communion has varied enormously from age to age and place to place. The instinct of the early church was twofold:

1. The Eucharist was not celebrated on fast days;

2. The fast on these days was ended with communion—from the reserved sacrament.

Only the Byzantines hold consistently to this ancient tradition today. In general, the full Eucharist was the way in which the West finally decided to conclude its fast, celebrating the sacrament at the end of the day (after nones). But on Good Friday, a full Eucharist did not seem appropriate, and so the ancient custom of receiving communion from the reserved sacrament was retained on this one day only— although for centuries it was only the celebrant (and not the whole congregation) that received. In the post-Reformation Church of England, however, the Holy Eucharist as a memorial of Christ's death and passion was considered peculiarly appropriate to this day, which was for centuries a major communion day. Only in the last century did Anglicans come to feel that a celebration was inappropriate. Today, usage varies in the Anglican Communion. The Anglican Church of Canada makes provision in the *Book of Alternative Services* for either a full celebration or communion from the reserved sacrament and requires neither. Both practices are current in the

Church of England. The American *Book of Common Prayer* 1979 provides only for communion from the reserved sacrament. We might do well to think of the Maundy Thursday celebration as the Eucharist that relates to Good Friday and to observe only the Ministry of the Word and the Adoration of the Crucified on Good Friday.

Preparation

On this day the altar is customarily bare and no candles are on the altar or elsewhere when the service begins. Participants vest in albs; they may also wear stoles of passiontide colors. The celebrant may wear or omit the chasuble. If communion is to be received, it will be from elements reserved on Maundy Thursday. Vessels and linens for the administration of communion will need to be laid out on the credence. For the Adoration of the Crucified a wooden cross or crucifix will need to be available to be brought to the chancel for this part of the service. Alternatively, a large wooden hanging cross, if such is in use in the church, veiled (as it would be for Lent), may be unveiled at the appropriate point in the service. Music for much of the service is found in *The Altar Book* and the Hymnal, as noted below. A setting for the entire rite is available from Mason Martens; this music gives the setting for the Passion. Traditionally the organ is not used on this day, but if it is necessary to support congregational singing, it should by all means be used—with a restrained registration.

The Liturgy of the Passion (Ministry of the Word)

The apparent austerity of this rite derives not from the character of Good Friday, but from the fact that as a "solemn season" it faithfully preserves the original simplicity of the early Roman Rite. *No music is appropriate during the entrance,* which is made in silence (without cross or torches) and concluded, after silent prayer before the altar, with the *Good Friday acclamation and the collect.* Music for this is found in *The Altar Book* and in the Hymnal at S 348.

An Old Testament reading, psalm, Epistle, and Gospel are provided. *Gradual Psalms* has a setting of the alternatives for Gradual Psalm, verse, and tract. A passion hymn would be appropriate as a *sequence* before the Gospel, which is John's Passion. The Passion on Good Friday is treated like the Palm Sunday Passions: no responses are made to its announcement or conclusion, the people may remain seated until the place where the rubric bids them rise, and the Passion may be read in parts, whose readers need not be ordained. Music for the Passion is available from Mason Martens. *The sermon,* the preaching of the passion, merits careful and extensive treatment. *A hymn* may follow the sermon on this day; the creed is omitted.

The Prayers of the People

The solemn bidding and collects are the most ancient Western form of the Prayers of the People. The full form for each category was originally a bidding by the celebrant (the Prayer Book now suggests that it may be made by the deacon), a period of silent prayer (opened by the bidding to kneel and closed by the bidding to rise), and the collect. Directions and music for this full ancient method of intercession are found in *The Altar Book.* If this seems unduly fussy or elaborate, the people may either stand or kneel throughout. The indented portions of each bidding may be adapted as local circumstances require. Deacon and celebrant may lead the solemn collects from their seats, or from whatever positions are customary for the Prayers of the People.

A hymn or anthem may now be sung, and the service concluded with the Lord's Prayer and *the final prayer* (music in *The Altar Book*), or it may continue with the Adoration of the Crucified.

The Adoration of the Crucified

At this point a cross is brought in, or a cross already in place is unveiled. The cross used should be a wooden one or a crucifix; it should not suggest the triumph of the resurrection. It may be accompanied by acolytes with candles, which may then be placed beside it or on the altar. The Lutheran *Manual on the Liturgy* suggests that three stations be made with it, at the same place stations will be made with the Paschal Candle at the Great Vigil of Easter. Two sets of versicle and response are provided in the Canadian *Book of Alternative Services* which might be used at the stations, or when the cross is in place:

> V. This is the wood of the cross,
> on which hung the Savior of the world.
> R. Come let us worship.
> *or*
> V. Christ our Lord became obedient unto death.
> R. Come let us worship.

Devotions before the cross then follow. An appropriate devotion not found in the Prayer Book is the ancient responsory known as the Improperia, or Reproaches. This was not printed in its traditional form in the Prayer Book, perhaps because it might be interpreted in an anti-semitic way. *From Ashes to Fire,* Supplemental Worship Resource 8 (Abingdon, 1979), presents a contemporary form of this responsory which is not subject to anti-semitic interpretation and might well be used in this place. The response used throughout this form is the Trisagion, for which music is found in the Hymnal at S 99–102 and S 360. Three other anthems are printed in the Prayer Book; music for them is found at S 349–351. Following the anthems the Prayer Book rubric directs:

> The hymn "Sing, my tongue, the glorious battle," or some other hymn extolling the glory of the cross, is then sung.

This hymn is found in the Hymnal at 165 and 166; a special form, traditional for this rite, is found at S 352.

The traditional form of the adoration, approaching the cross during these anthems with a triple genuflection and kissing it, is probably inappropriate for modern sensibilities. It is perhaps preferable for the people to kneel or sit while the anthems and hymn are being sung or said. The service may conclude after the adoration with the Lord's Prayer and the final prayer, as above.

Communion from the Reserved Sacrament

If communion is to be received, during or after the hymn the deacon (or an assisting presbyter or the celebrant) spreads a corporal on the altar, prepares the table with the vessels necessary for administration of communion, and brings the sacrament without ceremony from the place of reservation. The service then continues with *the Invitation, Confession, and Absolution* (from Rite II, unless the service is being conformed to the language of Rite I), *the Lord's Prayer* (which may be sung as at the Eucharist), *the sentence of invitation,* and *the administration of communion.* An appropriate hymn, psalm, or anthem may be sung during communion, or silence may be kept. After communion, the service concludes with *the final prayer* (for which music is found in *The Altar Book*). Then all depart in silence.

Holy Saturday

The Prayer Book makes liturgical provision for a proper liturgy on Holy Saturday, in addition to the Great Vigil of Easter. The proper liturgy is a simple form of the ministry of the word. After *the entrance* (presumably made in silence and without cross or torches), the celebrant begins the service with *the salutation and collect of the day. Old Testament reading, psalm, Epistle, and Gospel* are provided. A setting of the gradual psalm, verse, and tract may be found in *Gradual Psalms.* Hymn 172 or 173 might be appropriate as a sequence. The Creed is omitted. After a suitable sermon, *the anthem "In the midst of life"* replaces the Prayers of the People on this day. Settings of this anthem may be found at S 379 (Rite I) and S 383 (Rite II). The service then concludes with the Lord's Prayer and the Grace. The altar should be bare for this service, as on Good Friday; Passiontide colors are used.

The Great Vigil of Easter

The Great Vigil of the Christian Pasch or Easter is the climactic liturgy of the Christian year and should be celebrated as such. It is the principal Easter service and the entire parish, as far as possible, should be involved in its celebration. Some suggestions for making this celebration the highlight of the year follow.

1. The vigil should be held at an hour that makes it possible for families with children to attend. Any time after sunset on Easter Eve is appropriate.

2. A festive meal, or a reception (perhaps potluck) with festive food and drink, might appropriately follow the vigil.

3. The service ought to be planned in such a way that as many as possible have a part in it. Parts for children are especially important. Activities specially planned for them might also follow the service. Choirs and acolytes should likewise have important parts to play in this service. If the choir performs its major Easter music on Easter Day, then the vigil is not the most important service of the year for choir members. Many lectors may be involved in the various readings of the service. Handbells would be appropriate to accompany some of the plainsong chants and for use in other ways.

4. The service should be designed for the maximum participation of the congregation; but this does not necessarily mean that no special parts will be assigned to the choir. They too have their part to play in the celebration.

Preparation

Planning for the Great Vigil needs to begin early in the year. Choir, acolytes, and other participants will need to be rehearsed in the roles they will play in this service. In particular, the opening responses need to be rehearsed ahead of time, as there is little light to follow the service at the beginning. Service leaflets should be detailed, in order to make this potentially complex service easy for the congregation to follow.

A fire will be laid, or a taper available, at the place where the service will begin. Candles should be set out around the church; others may be available, if desired, for distribution to the congregation. Torches and cross are not carried in the opening procession. If they are to be used later in the service, they should be in place in the chancel before the service. The font should be ready. The church should be fully decorated for Easter. Adequate light should be available for the cantor to sing the Exsultet and the lectors to read the lessons.

The Service of Light

This liturgy may be held at the back of the church with the people in their seats, or at another place (in the parish hall or outdoors), with all proceeding into the church behind the Paschal Candle once it is lit.

The service begins in darkness. The celebrant may briefly introduce the rite, using *the address* in the Prayer Book or similar words. Fire is kindled or a taper lit. If incense is to be used, the fire may be used to start the charcoal for the thurible.

The opening collect on page 285 or another appropriate collect (such as that for the lesson from Isaiah 4:2–6, if that lesson and collect are not used at the vigil) may then be sung or said. *The Paschal Candle is then lit* and the entrance procession forms. No cross or torches will be carried in this procession, but incense may be used. The deacon (or the celebrant, in the absence of the deacon) carries the candle at the head of the procession. Three stations are made as the procession goes into the church, using *the versicle and response* given. Music for this is found in *The Altar Book* and also in the Hymnal at S 68. At the end of the procession, the candle is placed in its stand (which may be beside the pulpit or elsewhere in the chancel or at the front of the nave) and other candles (except those on the altar) are lit from its flame. Artificial lighting may be turned on at this time as needed. If the whole congregation enters in the procession, it may be preferable for them to light their candles as the procession enters the church, rather than at the end of the procession. If incense is used, the Paschal Candle may be censed after it is placed in its stand. *The Exsultet* is then sung or said by the deacon or (in the absence of a deacon) by another person, lay or ordained. This text should be sung if there is anyone in the congregation who can be taught to sing it. Music is found in *The Altar Book,* with the responses in the Hymnal at S 69. If the congregation have received candles, it may be convenient for them to extinguish them at this point.

The Vigil Lessons

The vigil lessons form a separate liturgy of the word from the Eucharistic lessons which come later in the service. They may be introduced by the celebrant with *the address* provided or in similar words. Taken from the Old Testament, these lessons both review salvation history and serve as types of redemption and baptism. *A series of nine lessons* is given, each *with a psalm and a collect.* At least two of these lessons, and preferably more, must be read, and the lesson from Exodus must always be included. Silence may be kept after each lesson, and a brief comment or homily may follow any of the lessons. Presbyters present may divide the collects after the lessons among them; the collects may be monotoned or sung to either of the customary tones. The lessons may be monotoned or sung to the same tone as the lessons before the Gospel at the Eucharist. The psalms (and canticles suggested after some of the lessons in place of psalms) should be sung in some way that facilitates congregational participation. Responsorial settings for all of them are found in *Gradual Psalms.* They may also be sung to plainsong tones or Anglican Chant or Simplified Anglican chant, or to the tones in the *Lutheran Book of Worship.* Music for the Vigil is also available from Mason Martens.

Holy Baptism or the Renewal of Baptismal Vows

Holy Baptism or the Renewal of Baptismal Vows follows here or after the Gospel at the Eucharist. This is the traditional place. For baptisms, as many as possible should gather around the font. The traditional psalm, Psalm 42, may be used for a procession to the font, led by the Paschal Candle. A metrical setting of this psalm is found as Hymn 658. Or an appropriate Easter hymn, such as Hymn 199 or 200 might be used. The baptismal liturgy then starts with the presentation of the candidates. Alternatively, the presentation may take place in the chancel, and the procession to the font may take place later, before or during the petitions for the candidates for baptism. If the arrangement of the church permits, it is preferable to have the procession at the beginning of the baptismal rite at this service. Further notes on the baptismal liturgy will be found in the next chapter.

Even if there are no baptisms on this feast, baptismal vows should be renewed, using the form found in the Prayer Book on page 292. The seasonal invitation to the renewal of vows on page 292 may also be used in the baptismal rite itself at the point when the congregation is invited to join in the baptismal covenant on the bottom of page 303. Even without baptisms, it may be appropriate on this occasion to make the procession to the font for the renewal of vows, and the font may be blessed, using the form found in the order for the Consecration of a Church. The congregation may be aspersed with the baptismal water when it has been blessed.

When the liturgy of the font is completed, the procession returns to the chancel, led by the Paschal Candle. It is especially appropriate on this occasion that those baptized be presented with candles lit from the Paschal Candle; they will carry them in this procession. Psalm 23, a metrical version of it, or an appropriate hymn may be used for the procession. It was formerly customary to use the litany for this procession, with the Kyries at the end of the litany serving as the Kyries of the Eucharist. However, the Great Litany is rather penitential in tone for this occasion, and the Litany of the Saints is inconsistent with the Anglican rule of not invoking the prayers of the saints in public worship. The procession may also return to the chancel immediately after the baptisms; the prayer for the gift of the Spirit and the consignation will then be performed in the chancel. At the Vigil, it seems best to have the font as the visual focus for the whole baptismal rite, however, unless the location of the font makes this difficult.

A Note on the Vigil when the Bishop is Celebrant: If the bishop is present for the Vigil, the baptismal rite may conclude with the laying on of hands in Confirmation/Reception/Reaffirmation. In this case, after the vigil lessons the bishop will sit in a chair before the altar for the presentation of candidates and the baptismal covenant and the procession to the font will take place before or during the petitions for the candidates. After the baptisms, the procession will return to the chancel, and the bishop will administer the consignation, the baptismal laying on of hands and the laying on of hands in Confirmation/Reception/Reaffirmation from the chair in the chancel.

The First Eucharist of Easter

After the procession returns to the chancel, the first Eucharist of Easter begins with the *Easter greeting* (which is optional) or *the opening canticle* (the Gloria, the Easter Canticle, or the Te Deum). It is traditional to begin this canticle with a burst of music—children and others might be encouraged to bring bells to ring at this time (perhaps put safely out of temptation's way until they are needed on a table at the rear of the church), and an organ or brass fanfare would be an appropriate response to the Easter announcement that Christ is risen. Whichever canticle is used, it should be in a setting that the congregation can join in easily and with gusto! In the old Roman Rite, the organ was silent from Maundy Thursday until the church bells were rung as the organ took up its voice once more for the Gloria in excelsis of the Easter Vigil.

There is no Old Testament reading at this Eucharist, since a series of readings from the Old Testament was used at the vigil. After *the Epistle, the Alleluia* is intoned once again for the first time since the beginning of Lent. S 70 in the Hymnal provides a setting for the Easter Alleluia, which traditionally is sung three times by the cantor, the people repeating the music each time. *Psalm 114* is provided as the gradual psalm. A festive Easter hymn would also be appropriate as a sequence in this place. *The Gospel* then follows. For *the sermon,* it might be appropriate to read the Easter homily attributed to John Chrysostom, which is read in the Orthodox liturgy. Alternatively, this magnificent homily might be used as an invitation to communion, for it takes the form of an invitation to the Paschal feast. The Creed is omitted at this service, since the Vigil includes the Apostles' Creed in baptism or the renewal of the baptismal covenant. Baptism or the renewal of baptismal vows may in fact take place at this point in the liturgy (as in the reformed Roman Rite).

The Prayers of the People and the Peace follow, the Confession being omitted. On this day, the people should stand for the Prayers of the People (and other prayers in the rite).

The celebration of the Holy Communion proceeds in the usual way. The alleluias should be used with the fraction anthem, and should be added (here and throughout the season) to the dismissal. An Easter form of the blessing may be used.

The Book of Occasional Services provides a series of blessings for Easter foods which might be used at a festive dinner following the Great Vigil.

Other Proper Liturgies

The notes in this part of the chapter deal with other proper liturgies for which provision is made in either the Prayer Book or *The Book of Occasional Services*. All of these are related to the Eucharist as one of the "regular services" of the Church.

The Baptismal Vigils

Provision is made for vigil Eucharists on the other baptismal feasts besides Easter. The Prayer Book in rubrics with the collects for Pentecost and in the lessons printed in the lectionary provides for a baptismal vigil for Pentecost. *The Book of Occasional Services* makes similar provisions for baptismal vigils on the Feast of Christ's Baptism (the first Sunday after Epiphany) and on All Saints' Day or Sunday. In each case the order of service is as follows:

1. *The Order of Worship for the Evening* is used for the entrance rite. In place of the Phos hilaron the Gloria in excelsis may be used; however, since the Gloria in excelsis is in origin a morning canticle and the Phos hilaron an evening hymn, the latter is perhaps preferable at the vigil. The collect for the day then follows.

2. *The Ministry of the Word* has an expanded number of readings before the Gospel. A selection of readings from the Old Testament and the Epistles is given; for each reading an appropriate psalm or canticle is given as a response. At least three readings (instead of the customary two) before the Gospel are to be used. Note that in this service, unlike the Great Vigil of Easter, the lessons are incorporated into the Eucharistic Ministry of the Word. Note also that, unlike the Great Vigil of Easter, no collects are provided with the lessons.

3. *Baptism,* beginning with the presentation of the candidates, *or the Renewal of Baptismal Vows, follows the Gospel (and sermon).* Renewal of baptismal vows (either in the baptismal service or apart from it) may be introduced by a special invitation drafted to fit the feast. On Pentecost, this would relate baptism to the gift of the Holy Spirit; on the first Sunday after Epiphany, it would relate baptism to Christ's baptism and his manifestation as God's Son; in All Saints' Season it would relate baptism to incorporation into the church as the communion of saints. This invitation is found in the middle of page 292 if the Renewal is made apart from baptism, or on the bottom of page 303 if it is made in the context of baptism. As at the Great Vigil of Easter, the font may be blessed using the form from the Consecration of a Church even if there are no baptisms, and the people may be aspersed.

The Book of Occasional Services also provides a different type of vigil "on the Eve of Baptism." This is for use when the baptismal Eucharist will be held the next day. It follows the same format as the first two sections of the regular baptismal vigil, and then is concluded with one of the forms of prayer provided and a blessing or dismissal or both. On the eve of baptismal feasts, proper lessons will be used; lessons are provided also for other occasions.

The Candlemas Procession

The designation of Christ as "a light to lighten the Gentiles" in the Gospel for the feast of the Presentation led to the rite of blessing candles on this day (hence the name "Candlemas"), followed by a procession with lighted candles. *The Book of Occasional Services* provides a proper entrance rite for use at the Eucharist on this feast if desired. *The people,* or a representative group of them, *gather at a place apart from the church or,* if this is not possible, *in the narthex or at the door of the church. Unlighted candles are distributed to all.* The rite begins with the same *greeting and response* used in the Order of Worship for the Evening, and, while the *Nunc Dimittis* is sung in responsorial fashion, *the candles are lit. A collect* follows. The deacon (or in the absence of a deacon, the other person appointed) gives *the bidding for the procession,* which forms and makes its way into the church with *appropriate hymns, psalms, or anthems. Another collect* is provided for a station. *Psalm 48:1–2, 10–13, with an antiphon,* is provided for the last stage of the procession as it approaches the altar. The Eucharist then continues with the Gloria. Candles are extinguished after the collect for the day; they may be relighted after the dismissal as the people leave the church. Traditionally, a cope would be worn by the celebrant for the procession. It would be simpler, however, for the celebrant to use the same vestments for the procession as for the Eucharist. Incense may be carried in the procession if desired. Music for the Candlemas procession is given in the Accompaniment Edition of the Hymnal at S 340–343. This is an *optional* entrance rite for this feast; it is entirely appropriate to celebrate the Eucharist with the usual entrance rite on the feast, since the procession is in fact peripheral to the principal theme of the Gospel for the day.

The Rogation Procession

Rogation Days (days of supplication for fruitful seasons, which have customarily been marked with outdoor processions and appropriate hymns, psalms, canticles, anthems, readings, and prayers) are listed in the calendar as "days of optional observance." They may be observed at whatever time local conditions and the convenience of the congregation make advisable, according to the rubrics of the Prayer Book and *The Book of Occasional Services.* Traditionally, they are kept on the three days before Ascension Day. At times, the preceding Sunday has been kept as "Rogation Sunday," although the Sunday propers are used at a Sunday Eucharist. For the procession, *The Book of Occasional Services* suggests *psalms, canticles, readings, and prayers,* and provides *appropriate additional petitions for use with the Great Litany.* The readings and prayers are used during stations in the procession; the psalms and canticles, as well as hymns, are used between stations. Hymn 292 is proper to Rogation Days; the liturgical index in the Hymnal lists other appropriate hymns. The Great Litany is traditionally used as the procession enters the Church, where the service may be concluded with the Eucharist (in which case the Kyries of the Great Litany serve as the Kyries of the entrance rite and the Prayers of the People are omitted) or with other suitable devotions.

On a day other than a Sunday or feast, the Rogation propers listed under Various Occasions 19 may be used for the Eucharist. The procession may precede the Eucharist on a Sunday or a feast (though the rubrics of *The Book of Occasional Services* discourages this), but the propers will be those of Sunday. If the Great Litany is not used as the entrance rite for the Eucharist, *The Book of Occasional Services* provides *appropriate additional petitions* for Form V of the Prayers of the People. When no outdoor procession is possible, a Rogation Eucharist may begin in the Church with the Great Litany. Incense may be carried in the procession if desired. The officiant may wear a cope, or the vestments to be worn at the Eucharist if this is to follow.

Admission of Catechumens
and Enrollment of Candidates for Baptism

Persons interested in baptism as adults may, after a period of inquiry, be admitted as catechumens at any time. *The Book of Occasional Services* provides liturgical forms for use during the catechumenate.

The admission takes place at the Sunday Eucharist after the sermon or the Creed. The service proceeds as follows:

1. Those seeking admission come forward to the celebrant, who examines them.

2. The celebrant, having admitted them, says a blessing over them and signs each with the sign of the cross.

3. The persons admitted are remembered in the Prayers of the People.

During the period of the catechumenate, these persons are instructed at catechetical sessions, each of which the instructor concludes by laying a hand on each catechumen with prayer. A variety of prayers is provided for this.

Catechumens are enrolled as candidates for baptism at Easter on the First Sunday of Lent; those to be baptized on the First Sunday after Epiphany are enrolled on the First Sunday of Advent. After the Creed, the service proceeds as follows:

1. Candidates are presented by their sponsors.

2. An examination follows.

3. The names of the candidates are publicly written in a book kept for this purpose, in token of their being entered in the Book of Life.

4. A special form of the Prayers of the People is used, with petitions for the candidates.

During candidacy, the names of the catechumens are included in the Prayers of the People, and a special blessing is provided which may be used, especially on the third, fourth, and fifth Sundays of Lent, or the second, third, and fourth Sundays of Advent.

This liturgical recognition of candidacy for baptism as an adult is optional; pastoral sensitivity will indicate whether it is used in individual cases. The forms above are not to be used for those already baptized who are being prepared for Confirmation/Reception/Reaffirmation.

Other Seasonal Services

The Book of Occasional Services provides for other seasonal devotions and services, which are *not* proper liturgies or related to the regular services of the Church.

We will take brief note of these at this time. *The Book of Occasional Services* provides forms for *Advent and Christmas Festivals of Lessons and Music.* These are series of lessons interspersed with appropriate hymns, canticles, and anthems. They are prefaced by a seasonal bidding prayer and concluded with an appropriate seasonal collect and seasonal blessing. If used in the evening, they may be opened with the entrance rite of the Order of Worship for the Evening. Otherwise an appropriate hymn, psalm, or responsory might be used at the entrance. The ultimate origin of this paraliturgical service is the nine lessons and responsories of matins in the classical Roman office. For Christmas Eve, a versicle, response, and collect are provided for *a procession to the creche.* If a vigil is desired before the Christmas Eve Eucharist, the Festival of Lessons and Music and the Procession to the Creche may be used for this purpose.

For Epiphany and Easter, forms for *the blessing of houses* are provided. Each begins with a greeting and continues with an appropriate canticle and antiphon (The Magnificat at Epiphany) or psalm and antiphon (Psalm 114 at Easter). The rite continues with a seasonal collect, a prayer of blessing, and a seasonal blessing.

Vigils for New Year's Eve and All Hallows' Eve are also provided. The entrance rite of the Order of Worship for the Evening is used, and after the Phos hilaron or hymn the service continues with a series of readings, each with a psalm or canticle and a collect. A sermon may follow the readings. The Vigil for New Year's Eve may continue with an act of self-dedication and conclude with 1) the Great Litany or other form of Intercession; 2) the Te Deum or other hymn of praise and concluding prayers; or 3) the Holy Eucharist for the Feast of the Holy Name, beginning with the Gloria. The Vigil for All Hallows' Eve may conclude with the Te Deum or other song of praise and concluding prayers.

The Way of the Cross is a traditional processional devotion for which *The Book of Occasional Services* provides a form. The customary fourteen stations may be used, or only the eight biblical stations. Besides opening and concluding devotions, the book provides for each station:

> a common versicle and response;
>
> a biblical reading;
>
> a proper versicle, response, and collect; the Trisagion.

This is a processional service, moving between stations marked by crosses or representations of the scenes of Jesus' way of the cross. The Trisagion may be sung between the stations, or stanzas of appropriate hymns (such as the Stabat Mater, Hymn 159) may be used. Other parts of the service are not customarily sung, though it would be possible to use the ordinary tones for versicles and responses, lessons, and collects. The officiant might wear alb or cassock and surplice (with stole and cope, if desired).

Tenebrae is a form of matins and lauds used during Holy Week, "anticipated" by being recited on the prior evening. Its special feature is the gradual extinguishing of candles set on a special candelabrum. *The Book of Occasional Services* provides a form of this service for Wednesday in Holy Week. Complete directions are given for a full or abbreviated service. Many settings of tenebrae (originally sung to the plainsong of the Office) have been composed. Parishes which use this service may wish to adapt music from the traditional sources.

CHAPTER 5

Holy Baptism

By its new placement in *The Book of Common Prayer* 1979, Holy Baptism is set by the Episcopal Church in the context of the "regular services" of the Church, rather than as an "occasional office" or "pastoral office." By this new placement, the Episcopal Church has signified that it understands Baptism as not just a pastoral rite related to the life cycle of individuals, but as an essential part of the life of the church itself. Two rubrics, on page 312 and 298, indicate that baptism is closely integrated into the course of the "regular services" of the church year:

> *Holy Baptism is especially appropriate at the Easter Vigil, on the Day of Pentecost, on All Saints' Day or Sunday, and on the Feast of the Baptism of our Lord (the First Sunday after Epiphany). It is recommended that, as far as possible, Baptisms be reserved for these occasions or when a bishop is present.*

> *Holy Baptism is appropriately administered within the Eucharist as the chief service of a Sunday or other feast.*

We have already seen, in the last chapter, that Baptism is an integral part of the Easter Vigil, and that *The Book of Common Prayer* and

The Book of Occasional Services provide special baptismal Eucharists for the vigils of the other baptismal feasts. In the light of all of this, we might best think of the baptismal Eucharist as the *proper liturgy* of baptismal feasts and an *appropriate liturgy* for other Sundays and feasts.

It should also be noted that Baptism is integrally related to the theology of these feasts. In Baptism, "we are buried with Christ in his death. Through it we share in his resurrection" (Easter). In Baptism, like Christ, we are "anointed by the Holy Spirit" and so empowered for the tasks to which God calls us (Pentecost). As Christ at his baptism was manifested as God's Son by birthright, so in our baptism we are "reborn by the Holy Spirit" and "are made [God's] children by adoption and grace" (Epiphany). By Baptism we are "incorporat[ed]... into [God's] holy Church, and...[made] worthy to share in the inheritance of the saints in light" (All Saints' Day or Sunday). Sunday itself is an appropriate occasion for Baptism because of its relation to Christ's death and resurrection (Preface 2 of the Lord's Day) and to the paschal and pentecostal gift of the Spirit (Preface 3 of the Lord's Day). The Creed as the Baptismal Covenant gives expression to these theological truths of Baptism. The invitation to join in renewing this covenant (on the bottom of page 303) should be cast on each of these feasts to highlight the aspect of baptismal theology to which the feast is related.

Participants

The baptismal rite presupposes the full assembly of the church with its various orders of ministry. The rubric specifies:

> *The bishop, when present, is the celebrant; and is expected to preach the Word and preside at Baptism and the Eucharist. At Baptism the Bishop officiates at the Presentation and Examination of the Candidates; says the Thanksgiving over the Water; [consecrates the Chrism]; reads the prayer, "Heavenly Father, we thank you that by water and the Holy Spirit;" and officiates at what follows.*

In the bishop's absence, a presbyter presides as the bishop's deputy;

the use of chrism consecrated by the bishop (which is to be desired, though it is not required) expresses the link to the bishop.

A presbyter not only presides in the bishop's absence but also, if the candidate's pastor, should (even in the bishop's presence) perform the baptismal action. A deacon might lead the prayers for the candidate(s) and, if the pastor of a candidate, perform the baptismal action. In cases of necessity, deacons and lay persons may officiate at Baptism, but may not say the prayer over the candidates after Baptism or perform the laying on of hands and consignation or use chrism. These parts of the baptismal rite will be performed for those baptized by deacons or lay persons at the next public Baptism at which a bishop or presbyter presides. Lay persons act as sponsors, ordinarily read the lessons which precede the Gospel, and present the oblations of bread and wine. At baptisms, it is particularly appropriate for sponsors to perform these last two functions at the baptismal Eucharist and to lead the prayers for the candidates before the Baptism.

Preparations

Out of Easter Season, the Paschal Candle should stand at the font and be lit for Baptism. In Easter Season, the candle leads the processions to and from the font.

Ideally, the font is a shallow pool of water into which the candidates may walk, with a source of water flowing in from above. In the classical rites, the candidates were baptized when their heads were held beneath this flow of water from above. Few churches will have this ideal layout, or the dressing room nearby which it necessitates. Our baptismal rite itself does not really make adequate provision for this kind of baptism, for time must be allowed when baptism is administered in this way for those baptized to clothe themselves in dry garments before joining in the rest of the Eucharist. The lessons of the baptismal vigils originally "covered" this time; in the Byzantine liturgy, the reading continues until the patriarch is ready to enter the eucharistic assembly with the newly baptized.

If the church has a standing font instead of a baptismal pool, as most churches do, a large ewer of water should be at hand to pour into the font. Newer fonts might best be constructed with a source of continuously flowing water. The following items should also be available near the font or pool:

• a shell or small pitcher to pour the water in Baptism, though an infant may be partially immersed or "dipped" even in a standing font;

• towel(s) to dry candidates after Baptism;

• oil to be consecrated for chrism when a bishop is present, or consecrated chrism on other occasions;

• candle(s) to be given to those baptized.

• a service book;

• certificates to give candidates and sponsors.

If consignation takes place in the chancel rather than at the font, then the chrism and certificates will need to be available there rather than at the font.

If the bishop is present to preside, then a chair for presiding should be placed in the chancel at an appropriate place before the altar (it will be moved to the side at the time of the offertory). Vigil liturgies have their own special preparations; in particular, the candles to be used for the service of light (at either the Easter Vigil or at the Order of Worship for the Evening at other vigils) need to be ready at hand.

The Entrance

The Easter Vigil and the other baptismal vigils all have their own proper entrance rites. At other baptismal Eucharists, the entrance is made as in the standard rite during a hymn, psalm, or anthem. This entrance song is properly related to the season or feast and to the propers rather than to baptism. After the acclamation, a special set of baptismal versicles replaces the ordinary entrance canticle (the Kyrie,

Trisagion, Gloria in excelsis or other hymn of praise). Music for the versicles is found in the Hymnal at S 71–74. If desired, however, the Gloria may follow these versicles, but it is better omitted on ordinary occasions. Note that the Collect for Purity, Summary of the Law, and Decalogue are not to be used with this rite. The salutation and collect for the day follow the baptismal versicles (and the Gloria, if used). Ordinarily the collect (and propers) for the day are used. When the bishop is present, part or all of the baptismal propers (Various Occasions 10) may be used (but preferably only on Sundays after Epiphany and Pentecost—those in "ordinary time"—and on weekdays which are not major feasts).

The Ministry of the Word

The Ministry of the Word proceeds in the ordinary fashion at this point (except at the Easter Vigil, where the order of service is different and the baptismal rite begins with the presentation of the candidates). The sermon might well relate the theology of the feast or the propers to baptism. Note that the sermon may be preached later, after the Peace, if desired. This provision presumably was made to allow infants to be baptized early in the rite and then taken out to the nursery. The normal placement of the sermon—directly after the Gospel—is to be preferred unless some compelling necessity forbids. Infants belong in church, not in a nursery.

The Presentation, Examination, and Baptismal Covenant

Except when the bishop presides at Confirmation/Reception/ Reaffirmation in the baptismal rite, or when the font is poorly located for the celebrant to preside from it at this part of the rite, the celebrant, those involved with the baptism, their families, the children of the congregation, and others (the whole congregation, if space permits) are now led in procession to the font. If incense is customarily used, it may be carried in the procession. In Easter season, the Paschal Candle rather than a cross will lead the procession. The traditional psalm for this procession is Psalm 42, which might be sung in any of a variety of ways (responsorial settings are found in *Gradual Psalms* and James Barrett's *Psalmnary*), or in its metrical form (Hymn 658). The liturgical index in the Hymnal lists appropriate hymns for this procession. On the baptismal feasts, a hymn for the feast which relates to Baptism would be an appropriate choice (attention needs to be paid to which hymns are appropriate for the procession to the font and which are appropriate for the return to the chancel).

All would ordinarily stand if the presentations are made at the font. If presentations are made at the chancel, it is perhaps better for the celebrant or deacon to bid the congregation to be seated. The bishop, if celebrant, would be seated in a chair in the chancel for the presentations and what follows (up to the baptismal covenant); a presbyter would ordinarily stand to preside at the presentations. If the presentations are made at the font, the candidates, family, and sponsors will have gone there with the celebrant in procession; if they are made in the chancel, these persons come forward at this time. The form for the presentations for Baptism is found on page 301. At the Baptism of infants, the two questions at the top of page 302 are asked of parents and sponsors (godparents).

The six questions which follow, asked of candidates who can speak for themselves and of parents and sponsors of other candidates, are the ritual form of conversion as "turning" to Christ. They express the reorientation of life required in Baptism. The first three questions give expression to the renunciations (of "the spiritual forces of wickedness," "the evil powers of this world," and "sinful desires"—the devil, the world, and the flesh in the older and sometimes misleadng terminology) necessary for this reorientation. If the oil of catechumens is to be used, as Dennis Michno suggests in *A Priest's Handbook,* then the candidates should be anointed with it here, for it is meant to give strength for wrestling with the powers of evil just renounced. However, the Prayer Book makes no mention of it, it has never been a customary Anglican usage, and its use is best omitted as an unnecessary ceremonial action peripheral to the rite. The next three questions (the "adhesions" or acts of adherence) give expression to the candidate's new allegiance to Christ. In the Byzantine Rite, all this is symbolized by making the renunciations facing the West (the region of darkness) and then turning toward the East (the direction of the rising sun) for the adhesion to Christ. In some situations, particularly when adult candidates have been involved in a liturgical catechumenate, this actual physical "turning to Christ" might be incorporated into the ceremonial action of the rite to advantage.

When the bishop presides, candidates for Confirmation/Reception/ Reaffirmation now rise and are presented by the minister (and sponsors). They are asked to reaffirm their renunciation of evil and to renew their commitment to Christ.

Next the congregation (which is bidden to rise if it has been seated until this time) is asked to support the candidates for Baptism (and Confirmation) in their new life in Christ.

The Baptismal Covenant follows, initiated by a bidding which may relate Baptism to the theology of the feast or occasion (as we saw above). The congregation joins in affirming the covenant in response to the celebrant's questions. The covenant takes the form of the three paragraphs of the Apostles' Creed in response to questions by the celebrant, followed by questions related to the living out of the Christian faith. The Creed was the original baptismal formula: candidates were immersed, or water poured over their heads, after they responded to each of the three questions. The Creed is in fact not an abstract theological statement, but a description of the new relationship with God entered through Baptism. The Canadian *Book of Alternative Services* and the *Lutheran Book of Worship* place the covenant directly before the baptismal immersion or affusion in order to reunite the ancient verbal form of the sacrament with the sacramental action—an order which is perhaps to be preferred to that in our book, where the prayers for the candidates and the Thanksgiving over the Water are placed between the covenant and the Baptism.

Prayers for the candidates now follow. They might be led by a deacon or by one of the sponsors or family. If the presentation and examination has taken place in the chancel, the procession to the font takes place now. This may be done during the prayers, but saying or singing the prayers during the procession may prove distracting, and the procession might better be made before the prayers, using a psalm or hymn as suggested above. Music for the Prayers and the Concluding Collect (always said or sung by the celebrant) is found in *The Altar Book,* with music for the responses in the Hymnal at S 75.

The Thanksgiving over the Water

The Thanksgiving over the Water follows. If a baptismal pool is used, it will already be filled with water, as will a standing font with running water. Otherwise, water is poured into the font from the ewer at this point. Large quantities of water should be poured; small amounts symbolically trivialize the importance of the rite. The pouring should be a visible, noisy action. It may be done by the celebrant or by some other person—perhaps a sponsor or family member or one of the children of the congregation. At the opening dialogue, the celebrant uses the customary gestures, and for the prayer the orans position. The water is touched (and may be signed with the cross) at the words, "now sanctify this water." Hands should be joined for the concluding doxology. The music for this prayer (set to the preface tone) is found in *The Altar Book*; the people's responses are at S 75 in the Hymnal. After the thanksgiving, the font may be censed if incense is used.

The Consecration of Chrism

The bishop, if present, may then consecrate the chrism. Perhaps it is most convenient if a quantity of olive oil (traditionally mixed with oil of balsam or other perfumed oil) is in a small glass pitcher or boat, from which it may later be poured into sealed containers. The bishop would use the orans position, touching the container (and making the sign of the cross over it, if desired) at the words, "we pray you to consecrate this oil." The music for this prayer is found in *The Altar Book.* Leonel Mitchell suggests prefacing the blessing with the bidding given for the consecration of chrism in *The Book of Occasional Services.* The only use for chrism authorized by the Prayer Book is for the consignation in Baptism. In older traditions it was also used in Confirmation, Ordination, and the Consecration of a Church and an altar. In the present Prayer Book rite for Confirmation, its use in Confirmation is to be avoided, lest it give the impression that the Holy Spirit is conferred by that rite rather than in Baptism; the other uses are also probably best avoided. In the present Prayer Book, chrism is meant to express the initial gift of the Spirit, not later strengthening by the Spirit. Chrism may be consecrated by the bishop on a visitation when there is no Baptism or at a diocesan service; in these cases, *The Book of Occasional Services* directs that it be consecrated after the Postcommunion Prayer.

The Baptism

The Baptism itself is best performed by the minister, whether presbyter or deacon, who has pastoral care of the candidate. A variety of circumstances will determine how Baptism is administered. The ancient form was to have the candidate step down into a shallow baptismal pool and to immerse the head under water running in from above, or to pour water over the head three times. Since the Reformation, those churches that practice adult baptisms have generally used full immersion, with the minister going into a deeper pool with the candidate and immersing the candidate completely under the water as he or she bent down. An infant may be partially immersed or "dipped"; in this case, the head should be kept above the water. This kind of Baptism, formerly traditional for infants (it is the preferred form for the healthy child in the 1549 Prayer Book) is possible with a large standing font. Adults or older children who are immersed will need special clothing for the rite, and will need to dress in dry clothing afterwards. An infant immersed will need to be at least partially stripped of clothing, dried, and reclothed. It was originally at this point that babies were clothed in christening gowns. Parents used to bathing their children will know that a completely naked infant is likely to "foul" the font. When affusion or pouring is the method used, an infant is held over the standing font by minister, parent, or sponsor, and older children and adults bend their head over the font while the water is poured. Whatever minister performs the Baptism says the baptismal formula.

Each candidate after Baptism may be presented with a candle lit from the Paschal Candle. Anciently, "enlightenment" was one name for Baptism; the presentation of the candle signifies that one baptized has received the light of Christ. In the case of infants, the candle will be presented to a sponsor. If the entire rite is performed at the font, the presentation of the candle may follow the postbaptismal prayer and consignation. If these actions are performed in the chancel, however, the candle will of necessity be presented immediately after the baptismal action.

The Consignation

Baptism is followed by a prayer for the gift of the Spirit and a formula used for the sealing (also known as the consignation). In the sealing the celebrant lays a hand on the person baptized and signs the forehead with the cross (using chrism, if desired). These actions may be done at the font. If several candidates have been baptized, the rubric permits reversing the order of the actions and sealing each candidate immediately after baptism. The prayer is said "over" the newly baptized—that is, while the celebrant extends hands over those who have been baptized. If desired, it might be monotoned or sung to one of the collect tones. If only one person is baptized, the celebrant might lay hands on during this prayer. These words and actions are restricted to a bishop or presbyter; if a deacon or lay person officiates, a bishop or presbyter performs them on the person baptized at the next public baptism in the parish. When these actions are completed, the congregation, at the celebrant's bidding, joins in welcoming the newly baptized.

These words and actions give expression to the gift of the Spirit in Baptism. They are, however, perhaps best understood as significatory rather than instrumental in this: from this perspective it is water

Baptism itself that confers the gift of the Spirit, as the formula for the consignation makes explicit. Holy Baptism, a rubric states, "is full initiation by water and the Holy Spirit into Christ's Body, the Church." Nonetheless, it cannot be said that there is theological consensus on this issue, and the consignation is an integral part of the liturgical action of Baptism in the present rite. In the present Prayer Book, as in the service in the Canadian *Book of Alternative Services* and the *Lutheran Book of Worship* these post-baptismal rites are textually nearly identical to the present Roman Catholic rite of Confirmation. That means that the present rite of Confirmation is not to be understood as it was in ancient liturgies (when still a part of the baptismal liturgy), as the portion of the baptismal liturgy which bestowed the gift of the Spirit; but rather as a strengthening by the Spirit when someone already baptized makes a mature commitment.

These post-baptismal rites may also be done in the chancel. In that case, after the baptism a procession returns to the chancel. Psalm 23 may be used for this procession; responsorial settings for this psalm are found in *Gradual Psalms* and James Barrett's *Psalmnary,* other settings may be used, or a metrical version may be sung (several are found in the Hymnal). A baptismal hymn might also be used, or an appropriate hymn for the feast. The liturgical index in the Hymnal should be consulted for suggestions. Adult candidates might kneel at a rail for the prayer and the consignation, and the celebrant might pass down the rail for the consignation. If these actions take place at the font, the procession will return to the chancel afterwards, and the same music may be used.

Confirmation / Reception / Reaffirmation

When the bishop is celebrant, Confirmation/Reception/Reaffirmation may now follow. The candidates for these rites will have been presented earlier. All three are variants of the same rite and have the same basic meaning: "receiv[ing] strength from the Spirit through prayer and the laying on of hands by a bishop" upon expression of "a mature commitment to Christ" (Catechism, page 860). The form of words used when the bishop lays on hands is determined by the context: Confirmation for those making a mature commitment for the first time; Reception for those who have made a mature commitment in another denomination; Reaffirmation for those baptized by a presbyter as adults and for those returning to the practice of their faith after a post-confirmation lapse. Although the rubric requires the laying on of hands only with the first formula, the present canon implies its use with all three formulas (if hands are not laid on, the act does not confer "confirmed" status), and this was the original intention of the drafters of the rite.

The customary practice is for the bishop to stand for the opening prayer of this section, with the candidates kneeling in front. The bishop may extend hands over the candidates for this opening prayer (and also the concluding one) or use the orans position. Extended hands are preferable. Then the candidates come forward one by one and kneel before the seated bishop, who lays hands on them. It is easiest if the candidate has a card with his or her name and hands this card to an assisting minister standing beside the bishop, who holds the service book and card for the bishop. Sometimes candidates come forward two by two, but this in reality saves little time and is to be discouraged. The card should indicate which formula is to be used. Someone may stand beside the bishop and hold the pastoral staff during this part of the rite. Alternatively, if candidates are kneeling at a rail, the bishop may move up and down the rail to lay on hands. When hands have been laid on all candidates, the bishop says the concluding prayer over them (using extended hands or the orans position). The bishop might use a monotone or one of the collect tones for the opening and concluding prayers; the formulas are perhaps better said.

The Peace

After the consignation (and the administration of Confirmation/Reception/Reaffirmation) the service continues with the Peace. The celebrant initiates the greeting and should then exchange it with the newly-baptized (and those who have received the laying on of hands). If the Peace was initiated from the font, the procession now returns to the chancel (see notes above for this procession).

The service then continues with the Prayers of the People or the Offertory. At the Prayers of the People, the proper collect for Baptism or Confirmation (with short ending) would be an appropriate concluding collect if not used earlier. Following the Prayers of the People, it might on occasion be appropriate to use portions of the Thanksgiving for the Birth or Adoption of a Child (probably the briefer form). The newly-baptized, their sponsors, and/or the newly-confirmed may present the bread and wine at the offertory. In the Great Thanksgiving, the Preface for Baptism may be used except at a principal feast. On Sundays in Ordinary Time the third Preface of the Lord's Day is also especially appropriate. If for some reason there is no celebration of the Holy Communion, an alternative ending is provided. The omission of the celebration would be appropriate only if the celebrant is not a bishop or presbyter, or in the case of an emergency baptism (when even the full baptismal rite might not be used). In emergency baptism of adults, it might be appropriate under some circumstances to administer communion from the reserved sacrament.

CHAPTER 6

The Celebration of the Holy Communion

The Celebration of the Holy Communion is the second major part of the Holy Eucharist. There are four basic actions or sections of this part of the service:

1. Taking the bread and wine (the Offertory);

2. Offering Thanks (the Great Thanksgiving);

3. Breaking the Bread (the Fraction);

4. Sharing the Bread and Wine (the Communion).

The Offertory and the Communion have no separate headings in *The Book of Common Prayer*. These actions should proceed without the intrusion of extraneous material. The greatest change from the prior editions of the Prayer Book was taking the Prayers of the People and the Confession out of the Offertory, so that the four actions would follow directly after each other. The visual focus of this part of the service is the altar table, around which the people are gathered for the sacramental meal. The notes on preparation for the service in chapter 3 cover this part of the service as well.

Participants

At the Celebration of the Holy Communion, the principal celebrant is *the bishop or presbyter* who *presides* at the table for the Great Thanksgiving. *Other (bishops and) presbyters may stand at the table* as concelebrants *and also assist in the distribution of communion. Deacons will set the table at the Offertory (assisted by others as necessary), bring additional vessels as needed at the fraction, assist in administering communion, perform the ablutions, and give the dismissal.* In the absence of deacons, assisting presbyters or the celebrant may set the table, assist with ablutions, bring the vessels at the fraction, and give the dismissal. *Lay persons normally collect and present the alms and present the bread and wine.* In the absence of sufficient numbers of ordained ministers, *lay eucharistic ministers* may assist in distributing communion (only the cup, at present). *Vested lay persons may also assist* at the altar as servers (acolytes). *A cantor may lead the memorial acclamation* during the Great Thanksgiving (the people repeating each phrase) *and a responsorial fraction and/or communion anthem. The choir leads the congregation in the Sanctus* and may also perform some of the cantor's functions. Choir anthems may be performed during the offertory or during communion. The choir leads the congregation when other hymns are used at the offertory and during or after communion.

Ceremonial Notes

Chapter 1 gives general notes on ceremonial actions and gestures; further details will be given below in regard to each section of this part of the Eucharist. The Offertory and ablutions are functional actions, and ceremonial elaborations are to be avoided at those places. Gestures during the Great Thanksgiving are basically rhetorical gestures and should not in themselves be given consecratory significance, but should be related to the text of the prayer.

If incense is used, the action should be kept simple. The following usage is suggested, if desired:

1. The altar, gifts, ministers, and people may be censed at the end of the Offertory.

2. During the Great Thanksgiving, the thurifer may stand gently swinging the thurible as a sign of the prayer being offered.

3. Incense may be carried in the final procession.

Elaborate ways of censing objects and persons should be avoided: censing should not interrupt the basic action of the service. Further notes are given below.

Music

The following parts of the service are normally sung when music is used:

> **Offertory:** hymn, psalm, or anthem
>
> **Sanctus/Benedictus**
>
> **Fraction anthem:** Pascha nostrum, Agnus Dei, or other anthems (confractoria)
>
> **During communion:** hymns, psalms, or anthems
>
> **After the Postcommunion Prayer:** hymn

Music is also available for these parts:

> **The Dialogue and Prefaces**
>
> **The entire Eucharistic Prayer**
>
> **The Memorial Acclamations**
>
> **The Doxology of the Eucharistic Prayers and the Amen**
>
> **The Lord's Prayer**
>
> **The Short Form of the Invitation to Communion**
>
> **The Postcommunion Prayer**
>
> **The Blessing**
>
> **The Dismissals**

With few exceptions, this entire portion of the service may be sung, and the Catholic tradition would be to do so. Evangelicals are likely to prefer to restrict music to hymns where the rubrics allow them, anthems at the Offertory and communion, and the Sanctus/ Benedictus and Agnus Dei in service music. At times, what is essentially a said service with hymns may be appropriate. Instrumental music during the Offertory, communion, and final procession is both permissible and common.

1. *The Offertory*
The People and Priest Prepare the Table.

A rubric notes that necessary announcements may be made before the offertory.

The rubrics give this part of the service the name "Offertory," though that is a misleading name and some other contemporary liturgies avoid it. "Taking" is not the same as "offering." Properly speaking, "the people's offerings of bread and wine, and money or other gifts" are *presented and placed on the altar* at this point. The gesture of offering—lifting up—should be used not here, but when the text of the Great Thanksgiving verbally offers them.

The celebrant may initiate the Offertory with a sentence of Scripture (one of those printed on pages 343–344 or on page 376 or another appropriate one) or a bidding (see page 344 or 376). Care should be taken to avoid the use of a sentence with words (such as "brethren" or "men") which might be understood as gender-specific. The action may simply begin without announcement as well.

It is perhaps simplest to list the customary actions (those with an asterisk are customary in many places, but not found in the rubrics):

    1.* The celebrant may ceremonially wash the hands when an assisting minister or acolyte brings a bowl, a towel, and a pitcher or cruet of water. This is the primitive place for this action, and it interrupts the flow of the service less here than in the customary place after the offerings are received and prepared.

2. The deacon, an assisting presbyter, or the celebrant prepares the table by bringing to it the cloth (corporal) and the chalice (and paten, if bread is not to be consecrated in the vessel in which it is brought to the table). *The Altar Book* is also brought to the table at this time if it is not already in place, and the proper place found in the book.

3. Meanwhile, ushers collect the alms and those appointed go to the oblations table for the bread and wine (and water).

4. The ushers bring the alms and the others the bread and wine to the altar.

5. The deacon, the assisting presbyter, or the celebrant receives the alms and oblations, standing either before or behind the altar. Alms and oblations should be presented directly to these persons, not passed up through a chain of others.

6. The gifts are then prepared at the table: sufficient bread is placed on the paten—or placed directly on the corporal in the vessel in which it was presented. The wine may be presented already mixed with water. If not, water (brought in the procession or from the credence) is added to the wine in the vessel in which it is presented. The chalice is then filled and placed on the corporal. If more wine will be needed, the vessel is placed on the corporal for consecration. Gifts consecrated at the service may also be taken from the service to the sick and homebound; sufficient amounts should be prepared for this purpose. Alms may be received in a receiving basin and then placed on the altar. They may be left there or removed to the credence or the sacristy.

7.* When the table is prepared, the celebrant may cense it by circling it and may cense the gifts with simple swings. Then a thurifer may cense the ministers (as a group) and choir and congregation as groups.

The gifts may be brought in a formal procession led by thurifer and/or cross and torches. This is an essentially functional, practical action, however, and should not overshadow the Great Thanksgiving. For this reason it seems best for the presenters to come forward on their own and to omit incense, cross, and torches. Alms and oblations may be presented separately, but it is preferable to receive them together as one offering. Careful planning will allow the table to be prepared quickly when the bread and wine are received. The procession need not wait until the end of offertory music to come forward.

The offertory procession now common in the Episcopal Church and other churches represents the people's offering of their "life and labor" to God. It is a relatively modern manner of organizing the offering. In the classic Roman offertory procession, the people came forward individually to make their offerings. The classic Byzantine procession is a *clerical* transfer of gifts prepared before the service from the table of preparation to the altar. Neither is directly comparable to the present offertory procession.

While the alms are being collected and the table prepared, a hymn, psalm, or anthem may be sung. Instrumental music may also be used. Like the entrance and communion songs, this is basically music to "cover" the action. Originally, an antiphonal psalm sung by the choir and concluded by the celebrant with a collect was used here, as at the entrance and the communion. This eventually shrank to the antiphon alone. The sentences of Scripture with which we now initiate the Offertory were in some earlier Prayer Books to be said or sung to "cover" it. A hymn or instrumental music is perhaps best here. Although this has come to be a traditional place for an anthem, an anthem in this place tends to stop or delay the flow of action. What is required is "cover" music, not a performance piece. Communion is a better time for a choir anthem. The custom of using both an anthem *and* a presentation hymn should be avoided. Hymns used at the Offertory should be related to the theme of the Gospel, season, or feast, or should look forward to the eucharistic action.

Like the entrance, the Offertory is a part of the service that attracts "clutter" which distorts the shape and meaning of the rite. Note the following:

1. The rubrics make no provision for either a presentation hymn or a presentation sentence. *The Hymnal 1982* in fact does not print the "Doxology" as a separate hymn, because it has so frequently been misused in this way.

2. If the hymn or anthem does not entirely "cover" the action, silence or instrumental music may follow until the Great Thanksgiving begins.

3. If instrumental music is used, it should not build to a crescendo in such a way as to suggest that the presentation is the climax of the rite.

4. The rubrics of *The Book of Common Prayer* 1979 (unlike those of the 1928 Book) do not direct that the gifts be offered when they are presented. They should simply be received and placed on the table. Neither lifting them nor making the sign of the cross over them is appropriate.

5. The Prayer Book makes no provision for offertory prayers and none should be used. The rationale of this rite makes a collect like the Roman "super oblata" redundant, and the other offertory texts of the Roman Rite are in origin the celebrant's private devotions and are not (as Roman liturgists confess) appropriate as texts to be publicly recited.

6. The mixture of water and wine is a purely practical custom with no theological significance: it should not be ceremonially elaborated.

The textual focus of this part of the Eucharist is the Great Thanksgiving; the musical high point is the Sanctus; the reception of communion is the climax of the action. The Offertory should not be allowed to overshadow these. The tendency to make the elevation of the alms a climactic moment in music and ceremonial is not true to Catholic theology and is directly contrary to the theology of the Reformers. An overemphasis on the offertory gives a Pelagian cast to worship.

2. *The Great Thanksgiving*

The People and Priest offer thanks (make eucharist).

When the table is prepared, the bishop or presbyter who is the
celebrant comes to the center to preside at the Great Thanksgiving.
Other (bishops and) presbyters may stand beside the celebrant at the
table as concelebrants. At some diocesan services, there may be more
bishops and presbyters than can gracefully stand at the table. At such
times, only a representative number of those present will stand at the
table with the principal celebrant. Some of the others may stand
behind the concelebrants at the altar as a "crown" or semicircle
associated in the celebration, if space permits and the occason
warrants. The notes below presume that the celebrant will stand
behind a free-standing altar facing the people. When this is not
possible and the celebrant stands before the altar with the back to the
people, he or she will turn to address the people at the opening
dialogue, perhaps at the bidding to the Lord's Prayer (though this has
not been customary), and later in the service for the invitation to
communion, the bidding to the post-communion prayer, and the
blessing. Deacons may stand near the altar to the side. If there are no
concelebrants, the deacon(s) may stand beside the celebrant at the
altar. In some places it is customary for those who bring forward the
alms and oblations at the offertory to stand near the altar as
representatives of the congregation. In an earlier age it was customary
for all to draw near to the altar and gather in the choir for the
Celebration of the Holy Communion; this custom may still be
possible at some times and in some churches. Where it is not possible,
it is perhaps better not to distinguish those who bring forward the
alms and oblations from other lay persons. In certain pastoral rites, it
might be appropriate for certain persons to stand near the altar during
the Great Thanksgiving—the newly baptized or confirmed, those
making a special commitment to Christian service, those being
married (and others in the wedding party), and others in similar
situations. When this custom is followed, those standing near the altar
should not obstruct the congregation's view of the altar.

Since we understand the Great Thanksgiving as an integral unit, it is preferable for the principal celebrant to recite it alone, and for concelebrants to avoid saying or singing the words either in unison with the celebrant or in a low voice. Verbal concelebration is a late Roman tradition and not consonant with the tradition of the Early Church or the Orthodox East today. It is also distracting. At times, however, the concelebrants may be designated to say or sing certain parts of the Eucharistic Prayer in place of the principal celebrant. In early Anglican tradition, in fact, celebrants standing on either side of a table lengthwise in the choir might share the Eucharistic Prayer—one taking the dialogue and the preface, the other continuing at the Post-Sanctus. This might be appropriate when one presbyter in a parish cannot or prefers not to sing. The other presbyter can then take the sung dialogue and preface, and the "non-singer" can continue after the Sanctus. Another possibility is for concelebrants in Eucharistic Prayer D to divide the intercessions after the epiclesis among them. On the whole, however, it is preferable for the integrity of the service for one person to say or sing the entire Eucharistic Prayer. A unison recitation of the institution narrative is particularly to be avoided: this gives undue emphasis to one part of the prayer. We will note the celebrant's gestures during the prayer below; it is generally simplest and most graceful if the concelebrants stand with hands folded throughout the prayer. If further gestures are desired, however, they might extend a hand toward the gifts during the institution narrative and epiclesis; at the oblation, some might assist in lifting the gifts up in offering.

The Eucharistic Prayer is a single text, and its unity is best preserved if the celebrant keeps gestures (manual acts) simple and avoids changes in voice during the prayer. We will note gestures appropriate to all the Eucharistic Prayers first, and then those appropriate to particular texts.

At the salutation, the celebrant may open the hands in invitation, raise them at "Lift up your hearts," and then assume the orans position, which is the basic posture throughout the Eucharistic Prayer. In the course of the prayer, the celebrant joins the hands whenever the people join in the recitation of a text—at the Sanctus/Benedictus, at the memorial acclamations in Rite II prayers, and during the frequent responses of the people in the course of Eucharistic Prayer C. By joining the hands, the celebrant is "drawing the people in" to the recitation of a text. At the final doxology of each prayer, the celebrant joins the hands and bows the head. This is a place where the gifts have traditionally been lifted in offering; however, it seems better to use this gesture where the gifts are offered in the text rather than here. When the celebrant uses one hand to make a gesture (or to turn the pages of *The Altar Book*), the other should be placed on the altar or on the chest for grace of gesture. It has been customary to bow slightly during the Sanctus in reverence before God; however, since the people are now standing during this song, the bow might be omitted. It has also been customary to make the sign of the cross on oneself at the word "Blessed" in the Benedictus Qui Venit after the Sanctus. This would be appropriate if the text spoke of the worshiper being blessed; but the reference is almost certainly to Jesus in his incarnation in this context, so the sign of the cross is best omitted. Throughout this prayer *The Altar Book* should be in a position that is easy to read; for this reason it should be on a stand of sufficient height, and not flat on the altar (though it might look better on the altar in this way). It is also awkward for the celebrant to hold a small book during this prayer rather than to use an Altar Book, and this should be avoided.

In all the Eucharistic Prayers, a hand is laid on the bread and wine during the appropriate words in the institution narrative, or they are taken into the hands. Historically, it would be preferable to omit any gesture here (since the "taking" is done at the offertory); but a gesture is prescribed by the rubrics, so the celebrant should choose the less obtrusive one. In any case, no other gesture (such as signs of the cross, elevations, breaking the bread, bows, or genuflections) should be used. The function of the story in the eucharistic prayer is as a "warrant" for the rite, not as a consecratory formula: the best contemporary eucharistic theology would hold that we consecrate by giving thanks, so that the prayer as a whole consecrates, not some fixed text within it. The "taking, breaking, and giving" are done elsewhere in the rite (the offertory, fraction, and communion): they should not be duplicated in manual acts during the institution narrative.

The other basic gestures used are those of offering—the oblation—(lifting is the standard gesture for this, though laying a hand on the gifts and pointing to them are also possible alternatives), of invoking the Spirit—the epiclesis—(extending the hands over the gifts or laying hands upon them), and blessing (make the sign of the cross over the gifts). They should normally be made when the text of the prayer suggests, and we will look at the specific texts of each Eucharistic Prayer to see where the gestures are appropriate. They are basically rhetorical gestures—they highlight the meaning of what is being said in the prayer and are not in themselves necessary for "validity."

The hands are opened in invitation for the bidding to the Lord's Prayer, then joined once again as the people join in the prayer. There is, however, precedent for using the orans position during this prayer as well. A solemn bow may be made at the end of the Great Thanksgiving, or perhaps better at the end of the Lord's Prayer considered as the conclusion of the Great Thanksgiving, in reverence for Christ's presence in the gifts consecrated. It is inappropriate earlier in the text of the prayers.

In Eucharistic Prayer I, the gifts may be lifted in offering at the words "with these holy gifts, which we now offer unto thee." One or two signs of the cross may be made over the gifts at the words "bless and sanctify" and the hands extended over them through the remainder of this paragraph in invocation of the Spirit; or the sign(s) of the cross may be omitted and the hands extended throughout the whole paragraph. The celebrant might bow in self-oblation (with hands joined) during the paragraph which begins, "And here we offer and present unto thee...." If desired, the sign of the cross may be made on oneself as a sign of blessing received at the words "heavenly benediction." The celebrant may strike the breast lightly as a gesture of penitence at the words "although we are unworthy."

In Eucharistic Prayer II, the gifts may be lifted in offering at the words, "these thy holy gifts which we now offer unto thee." The sign of the cross may be made once or twice over the gifts at the words "bless and sanctify" and the hands extended over them during the rest of the paragraph; or the sign(s) of the cross may be omitted and the hands extended throughout the whole paragraph. The sign of the cross may be made on oneself at the word "benediction."

In Eucharistic Prayer A, the gifts may be raised in offering at the words "we offer you these gifts". The sign of the cross may be made over the gifts at the words, "Sanctify these gifts" and the hands extended over them for the rest of the sentence. Care should be taken not to rush the gestures in this sentence, and it may prove easier to omit one or the other of them. The sign of the cross may be made on oneself at the words, "Sanctify us".

In Eucharistic Prayer B, the gifts may be lifted in offering during the words beginning, "presenting to you". The hands may be extended over the gifts during the sentence beginning, "We pray you, gracious God." The sign of the cross may be made on oneself at the words "being sanctified." The names of appropriate saints may be inserted in the blank in this paragraph.

Eucharistic Prayer C has a different structure. The people have frequent responses (for which the celebrant joins the hands). The oblation and epiclesis both come before the institution narrative. The gifts may be lifted in offering at the words "bring before you these gifts;" the sign of the cross may be made over them during the sentence beginning, "Sanctify them". The use of this prayer is rendered problematic in some situations because of the phrase, "God of Abraham, Isaac, and Jacob," which gives a patriarchal cast to the text that some may find offensive.

In Eucharistic Prayer D, the gifts may be lifted in offering at the words beginning "offering to you". The hands may be extended over the gifts during the paragraph beginning, "Lord, we pray," and the sign of the cross may be made over them in this paragraph at the word "sanctifying". Appropriate names may be inserted in the commemorations after the epiclesis.

The use of the different Eucharistic Prayers of Rite II may follow seasonal themes: Prayer A, with its focus on cross and resurrection, seems especially appropriate to the Easter cycle of seasons; Prayer B seems appropriate to the Christmas cycle. Prayer C has a strong emphasis on creation and also on penitence, but seems better for occasional rather than regular use. Prayer D is an ecumenical text and is appropriate for ecumenical occasions; its longer text also seems suited to particularly solemn occasions.

An Order for Celebrating the Holy Eucharist also provides two partial forms which may be used in drafting eucharistic prayers. *In Form 1,* the gifts may be lifted in offering at the words, "We bring you these gifts". The sign of the cross may be made and/or hands extended in the sentence beginning with the words, "Sanctify them".

In Form 2, the hands may be extended in the paragraph beginning, "Send your Holy Spirit". Here there is no explicit textual offering of the gifts. For that reason, it would be appropriate in this case to lift them in offering during the final doxology.

Music is found in *The Altar Book* for the dialogue and all the prefaces in both simple and solemn tones. The dialogue is found in the Hymnal at S 112 (Rite I) and S 120 (Rite II). Settings for the Sanctus are found at S 113–119 (Rite I) and S 121–131 and S 364–365 (Rite II). Although the Benedictus Qui Venit is an optional text in Rite I in the Prayer Book, all the Hymnal settings of the Sanctus include it. The Rite II memorial acclamations are found in the Hymnal (sometimes with music for the protocol or introduction as well) at S 132–135 and S 366 (Prayer D). The entire Eucharistic Prayer may be sung. It is customarily set to the preface tone. Mason Martens has set the text of some of the prayers. Two settings of Prayer C (including responses) are found in the Appendix to the Hymnal at S 369–370. *The Altar Book* contains settings for both the whole doxology of the prayers and the concluding phrase of the doxology. Music for the final Amen is found at S 118 (Rite I) and S 142 (Rite II). Additional settings are found at S 143–147. Music for the bidding for the Lord's Prayer is found in *The Altar Book*; the traditional setting for the Rite I Lord's Prayer is at S 119 and settings for the Rite II text are at S 148–150.

3. The Fraction

The People and Priest Break the Bread.

The fraction is in origin a functional, practical action. The bread is broken that all may share. Secondarily, it is an acted memorial of Christ's death, his body broken on the cross (as it was an acted parable of his coming death at the last supper). When a leavened loaf is used, the full practical significance is apparent. When unleavened breads are used, at least one bread will be broken (and the pieces should be shared, not reserved for the celebrant). Concelebrants are to join, according to the rubric, in the breaking of the bread. If all unleavened breads are the same size, then all may be broken: this is probably preferable to a larger "celebrant's" bread and smaller "people's" breads.

Silence is kept when the action is begun. Then, particularly if much leavened bread is to be broken, a fraction anthem (confractorium) may be sung. (The anthem is *optional*, however.) It may prove convenient simply to break a loaf into smaller pieces at this time, and to break off individual portions during the administration of communion. The Roman Catholic practice of breaking a large bread into two pieces and then breaking off a small portion to mix with the wine is not in our rubrics and is perhaps best avoided. This commixture has had three meanings historically: 1) The Byzantines treat it as the reunion of Christ's body and blood in the resurrection—an artificial allegorical interpretation which has no place in our rite. 2) At Rome, a bread from the pope's mass was taken by an acolyte to parochial celebrations, where it was mixed with the gifts consecrated in the parish church—a sign of the unity of the eucharistic celebrations on that day—a practice which is possible only in small urban dioceses and has long since fallen into disuse. 3) When communion was received from the Reserved Sacrament (as on Good Friday), commingling of consecrated bread with unconsecrated wine was thought to consecrate the wine—in a full celebration, this is irrelevant, even if one agrees with this peculiar manner of consecration. Since none of these meanings obtain in our rite, the practice is redundant.

As soon as the bread is broken, other vessels necessary for the ministration of the sacrament are brought to the table and prepared for this purpose, breads being distributed and wine poured from the flagon or other vessel. This is the function of the deacon if present; otherwise an assisting presbyter or the celebrant will do this.

The short anthem Pascha Nostrum is printed in the text of both Rites I and II. It may be said or sung as a versicle and response (either the cantor or the celebrant singing the versicle) or sung as an anthem. Alleluia is to be omitted during Lent and sung during Easter Season; at other times, its use is optional (though probably desirable). Settings of this text are found in the Hymnal at S 151–156.

The traditional anthem in the West has been the Agnus Dei, originally repeated as many times as necessary to "cover" the action. The Agnus Dei is printed in the text of Rite I, though preferably it will be said or sung as an alternative (not an addition) to the Pascha Nostrum. It might be appropriate to non-festal or to penitential celebrations. In Rite II, it is printed not in the text, but in the Additional Directions on page 407. Settings of the Agnus Dei are found in the Hymnal at S 157–159 (Rite I), S 160–163 and S 373–374 (Rite II), and S 164–166 (Rite II, alternative text).

Other fraction anthems or confractoria are printed in *The Book of Occasional Services*; music for some of these texts is found in the Hymnal at S 167–171. In *The Book of Occasional Services,* anthems 11–15 and the psalm verses suggested for use with them are in actual fact more communion responsories than fraction anthems and would be appropriate during communion. S 172 is an example of this category in the Hymnal. It is also possible to use some of the other fraction anthems for this purpose.

In Rite I, the prayer of "humble access" may follow; it is optional, and it may be recited by either the celebrant or by the people in unison. It is customarily said kneeling, but those behind a free-standing altar will bow rather than kneel. It is a devotional text and should be said rather than sung. It is perhaps best used only in penitential seasons or omitted altogether.

4. *The Communion*

The People and Priest share the Gifts of God.

The communion itself is initiated by the celebrant's invitation, in either shorter or longer form (this verbal invitation is optional in Rite I). The shorter text may be sung to the music found in *The Altar Book*. The people should begin coming forward as soon as the invitation is given. A rubric in the Additional Directions stipulates that the celebrant receives "while the people are coming forward." Concelebrants and other ministers of communion may receive from the celebrant or from one another—the procedure should not be unduly protracted. Those at the altar receive standing.

The layout of the church will determine where the people receive and in what posture (standing or kneeling). At services with large numbers of communicants, additional stations may be provided to allow for the efficient ministration of the sacrament. At least one station should be accessible to the handicapped. A good rule is to provide, when possible, one station for every hundred communicants at large services. As the bread may be more easily distributed than the wine, two chalices may be assigned to every ministrant of the bread. Bread and wine are, according to the rubric, always to be available separately to all communicants. However, intinction may be allowed in a manner approved by the bishop. Separate intinction cups are to be avoided: they contradict the symbolism of the common cup. Communion should not take an undue amount of time. Careful planning will allow for efficient ministration of the sacrament, even at large services.

The rubric provides for hymns, psalms, or anthems during the ministration of communion. Silence or instrumental music is also appropriate. Eucharistic hymns and hymns proper to the feast or season are suitable here. Some of the canons at the end of the Hymnal are also possible selections. As noted above, some of the fraction responsories or confractoria are in fact more appropriate textually during communion. Psalm 34 is a traditional and appropriate text. Responsorial psalmnody is very ancient here, although at an early date it was replaced in the Roman Rite with an antiphonal psalm concluded by a collect (the same usage as at the entrance and the Offertory—the two other "processions" of this rite). This is also perhaps the best place for a choir anthem.

If necessary, additional bread or wine may be consecrated by a bishop or presbyter, using the form on page 408. This form should be said aloud, but softly. This usage is preferable to the other option, the repetition of a portion of the Eucharistic Prayer. It is also possible to use the reserved sacrament if elements consecrated at the service are insufficient. The rubric makes no provision for this common practice, however, because it is preferable to use elements consecrated at the service and the use of the reserved sacrament in this way is often abused. At large services, ministers may be assigned to bring additional supplies of consecrated bread and wine to the ministrants as necessary.

When the ministration of communion is completed, bread and wine are set aside for use by lay eucharistic ministers who will take the sacrament to the sick and shut-in immediately after the service and also reserved for communion of such persons at other times by the ordained ministers of the parish, for use in public worship by a deacon when no bishop or presbyter is available to preside at the Eucharist, and (on Maundy Thursday) for the Good Friday Communion. Then the remaining bread and wine are consumed by the celebrant and assisting ministers (and other communicants if necessary). The deacon (or in the absence of a deacon, an assisting presbyter or the celebrant) cleanses the vessels—preferably at the credence or in the sacristy. If it is necessary to perform these ablutions at the altar, this action should not be done facing the people. A rinsing with water is sufficient at this time. The vessels cleansed should then be set on the credence, not the altar. Ablutions may also be done after the dismissal. The rubrical provision of a hymn before the post-communion prayer is meant to "cover" this action if it must be done by the celebrant. The distinction between this hymn and communion hymns is more theoretical than real, however.

The post-communion prayer, led from the altar, follows. In Rite I, it may be said or sung by the celebrant alone (with hands in the orans position) or in unison with the people (in which case the hands will be joined, after they are spread in invitation at the bidding). If the celebrant sings the prayer, a monotone or one of the customary collect tones may be used. Rite II requires that the people join in this prayer. Proper post-communion prayers are provided for communion under special circumstances and celebrations with the sick, for marriages, for burials, and for ordinations and the celebration of a new ministry. All of these proper prayers *may* be said by the people; the rubrics *require* the people join in at the ordination of a bishop and the celebration of a new ministry. Candles are best extinguished directly after this prayer.

A hymn may follow the post-communion prayer. It may be a hymn appropriate to the feast or the season or an appropriate eucharistic hymn. The liturgical index in the Hymnal lists hymns particularly appropriate at this place. This hymn may be used for the final procession, although those who construe the rubrics literally frown on this custom. Surprisingly, "cover" music was not customary in liturgical tradition for this procession, although a hymn after a service has been customary in Anglican worship since the time of Elizabeth I. A rubric provides that necessary announcements may be made before the end of the service—that is, before the dismissal.

In Rite I a blessing will, and in Rite II it may, follow. In Rite II a deacon will, and in Rite I a deacon may, then dismiss the people. In the absence of a deacon, the celebrant or an assisting presbyter may give the dismissal. The rubrics specify only a deacon or the celebrant. A concelebrating presbyter might, however, be understood as within the scope of this rubric (as also might be the case with the rubrics for preparing the table and for ablutions).

A shorter and longer form of blessing is printed with Rite I, and blessings are printed for use at the ordination of bishops and presbyters. For Rite II, the celebrant may choose or draft a blessing; none is provided. *The Book of Occasional Services* provides seasonal blessings in threefold and onefold forms: they may be used with either rite. When a threefold blessing is used, it should probably be printed in the service leaflet, so that the people know when to respond with their Amens. In Rite II, the celebrant might also draft a blessing related to the season, the feast, or the propers. During Lent and Holy Week, *The Book of Occasional Services* provides Prayers over the People—the original form of blessing. The sign of the cross may be made over the people by the celebrant (current Catholic practice) or one or both hands extended over them (the ancient gesture and the Evangelical preference). This latter is the gesture that should be used with the Prayers over the People. Music for the blessing is given in *The Altar Book*. For Prayers over the People, a monotone or one of the collect tones might be used. Music for the versicles and responses of a bishop's blessing are found in the Hymnal at S 173. Rubrically, the post-communion hymn comes before this blessing; some prefer to place it after the blessing in order to give the blessing from the chancel and then to have "cover" music for the final procession.

The dismissal follows, and should in any case come after the post-communion hymn (so that it means what it says: "you can go now"). If it is not intended that the people leave, "Let us bless the Lord" should be used, since it is the one form which does not direct people to leave. Music for the dismissals is given in the Hymnal at S 174. In Easter Season, when a double alleluia may be added to the versicle and response, the music at S 175 or 176 is used.

A postlude of organ or other instrumental music may follow the service. When the ministers and choir have not left during the post-communion hymn, they may depart during this music. The procession may be organized in the same way as the entrance procession. Some may prefer to leave informally after the dismissal.

One common custom which "clogs" the end of a service is the ceremonial extinguishing of candles after the end of the final procession. People have been trained to remain in their places until candles have been put out. It is preferable to extinguish candles unobtrusively. This might be done by someone during the dismissal hymn, so that the dismissal does mean what it says.

Communion Under Special Circumstances

This rite is basically a form for the ministration of communion to those "who for reasonable cause cannot be present" at the parish Eucharist. At the present time, it may be used only by ordained ministers; a separate form has been issued by the Standing Liturgical Commission for use by lay eucharistic ministers, although there seems to be no good reason why they should not use the Prayer Book form (adapting the absolution and omitting the blessing as a deacon does). English and Canadian Anglicans use the same rite in both cases.

This is a brief rite appropriate for the seriously ill, for whom a longer form would be too taxing. For those who are shut-in but not seriously ill, it would be appropriate to add lessons from the propers, as rubrics allow, or to use a fuller form of the Ministry of the Word such as that on pages 453–455. When the shut-in receive communion in this way on a regular basis, it is desirable to read at least the Gospel from the Sunday propers.

The minister should follow the form in an orderly but relaxed manner. Postures should be appropriate to the circumstances. Any convenient table may be used to lay out the sacrament. The sacrament may be administered in one or both kinds, as parish custom and particular circumstances may suggest. For those with impaired vision, the form of confession most familiar should be used, and a copy of the form in large print should be available. The rite should be distinct from the rest of a pastoral visit, not mixed informally with it. If the location is close to the church, the minister might walk to the location in alb and stole or cassock, surplice, and stole after the parish celebration; otherwise, vestments are best omitted, though some may wish to wear a stole. If communion is administered in both kinds, a communion set with vessels of reasonable size should be used; miniature vessels trivialize the rite, as do ordinary dishes (except when circumstances necessitate).

Any regular communicant who is a shut-in has a right to weekly communion. While parish clergy may not be reasonably expected to administer the sacrament to a large number of shut-ins so frequently themselves, the canonical provision for lay eucharistic ministers should make this possible.

An Order for Celebrating The Holy Eucharist

For services other than the principal Sunday or weekly celebration of the Eucharist, *The Book of Common Prayer* provides the outline of a rite for which the texts may, in large part, be drafted by the participants. The descriptive sentences under the headings for each section of the Holy Eucharist in Chapter 3 and this chapter have been taken from that outline (which is a useful teaching tool). This rite has a wide variety of uses. Some of them might be:

1. It provides an appropriate form for an informal eucharist for small groups.

2. It provides a way to use a eucharist with a form of the Great Thanksgiving specially drafted for a particular occasion, such as a funeral or a wedding.

3. It provides a way for study groups to celebrate (with some adaptations) historic liturgies.

4. It provides a way to draft a rite appropriate for regular use at small daily celebrations (where the standard entrance rite, with canticle meant for singing, is unduly elaborate—a greeting and the collect would suffice).

5. It provides a way to draft a rite with particular concerns—such as a theological concern for greater sensitivity to inclusive language—in mind.

This outline, used thoughtfully and intelligently, can meet these as well as other needs.

The opening rubric stresses the need for careful preparation. The temptation to make up the service as one goes should be resisted.

Further Suggestions

The expanded format for the Ministry of the Word in this rite provides scope for a variety of art forms. The rubrics require a reading from the Gospel, and other art forms should be carefully integrated with the theme of the Gospel. Dialogue or discussion after the readings is appropriate in some situations, but it should be carefully planned.

If a special form of the Great Thanksgiving, using one of the Forms given on pages 402–404, is drafted, the drafting should be done with careful attention to the themes set out in the rubrics. A celebrant should work from a full text or a carefully prepared outline and not depend on spontaneous inspiration.

The rubrics allow the people to communicate each other, but this should be done in a reverent way, and the remaining elements reverently consumed.

If the Eucharist is celebrated in connection with a meal, the meal should be distinct from the Eucharist: the rubrics require that it follow the Eucharist. No attempt should be made to integrate the eucharistic rite itself into the meal.

If what is desired is a special eucharistic prayer, the service may be celebrated from Rite II in the Prayer Book with the properly drafted form of the Great Thanksgiving used for that printed in the text of Rite II.

The rubric on page 437 of the marriage rite and rubric 8 on page 506 of the Order for Burial make it possible to use a specially drafted Eucharistic Prayer at a Rite II marriage or burial.

Contents Chapter 7

The Pastoral Offices

We turn now to the Pastoral Offices in *The Book of Common Prayer* and related services in *The Book of Occasional Services*. Unlike the "regular" services which we have reviewed so far, the Pastoral Offices are keyed to events in the lives of individual Christians, not to the cycles of the day, the week, and the year. Pastoral Offices have always been included in editions of *The Book of Common Prayer*, though this has usually not been the case with service books of other denominations. By including these services in the Prayer Book, the church has declared its care and concern as a community for individuals at these important moments in their lives.

Confirmation / Reception / Reaffirmation

The concern of this rite is with individuals at such time as they are ready "to make a mature public affirmation of faith and commitment to the responsibilities of their Baptism and to receive the laying on of hands by the bishop," in order to be empowered by the Holy Spirit to live out that commitment. Normally, the bishop would administer this rite in the context of baptismal Eucharist on visitation to a parish. For convenience, the appropriate portions of the baptismal service are printed out here for use when the parish has no baptisms on the day of the visitation, or at a diocesan service. Notes in greater detail on parts of this service may be found in the chapter on Holy Baptism.

Preparation

A chair should be placed before the altar for the bishop to preside from at this service. It should be one which may easily be moved at the time of the Offertory. If chrism is to be consecrated for use at Baptism in the parish, olive oil mixed with perfumed oil (oil of balsam is traditional) should be ready for the bishop to consecrate in a small glass pitcher (from which it may later be poured into sealed containers). It may be on the credence or a table in the chancel, or it may be on the oblations table to be brought forward at the Offertory. Candidates for Confirmation/Reception/Reaffirmation are best seated in the front rows of the nave seating, with their sponsors seated nearby if desired.

The Entrance Rite and the Ministry of the Word

The entrance rite is that of Holy Baptism. As in that service, the acclamations are followed by special baptismal versicles and then by the salutation and collect of the day, although the Gloria in excelsis may be sung before the salutation if desired. Although special propers for Confirmation are provided in Various Occasions 11, there is no rubrical provision for their use on Sundays or Major Feasts. They might be used at a weekday Confirmation, a diocesan service, or a Confirmation on Sunday afternoon when the parish Eucharist has been celebrated in the morning. In this service, the Ministry of the Word concludes with the Sermon; the Nicene Creed is omitted.

Confirmation / Reception / Reaffirmation

After the sermon, the candidates are presented, either by their sponsors or by the minister or by both. The bishop is seated in the chair at this time and may hold the pastoral staff (or have another hold it beside the chair). It may be well to instruct the congregation to remain seated during the presentation and examination. Candidates and presenters stand for the presentation. Often it will be most convenient at this point if candidates stand in their places, though they may come forward and stand to either side of the bishop, along the communion rail if this is convenient. Different categories of candidates are presented separately.

After the candidates have been presented and examined by the bishop, the people are instructed to rise and all promise their support of the candidates and join with them in the renewal of the baptismal covenant. Prayers for the candidates follow, the people remaining standing and the candidates kneeling if circumstances permit. Silent prayer may follow the initial bidding, or the *petitions only* (and not the concluding collect) from the baptismal litany may be used. A deacon, presbyter, or lay person may lead these. This is *not* the place to insert other forms of prayer (such as the Prayers of the People). The silence (and petitions) are concluded by the bishop's prayer on page 418. This and the prayer after the laying on of hands may be monotoned or sung to a collect tone, if desired. The candidates then come forward one by one for the laying on of hands. Each has a card with name and a notation as to which formula will be used. An assisting minister receives the card and holds it for the bishop to read from. In the past, candidates have sometimes come forward two by two, but this in reality does not save much time, and somewhat depersonalizes the rite. Alternatively, the candidates may stay at the rail and the bishop may pass along it, laying hands on the candidates at the rail. If there are many candidates, the congregation may be seated for the laying on of hands. It is most appropriate to use the laying on of hands with all three formulas, although the rubrics require it only with the "Confirmation" formula. Notes on which formula should be used in individual cases are found in the chapter on

Baptism. Chrism should not be used for the laying on of hands in this rite; the text of the prayer of consecration indicates that its use is intended for Baptism only. After the bishop's final prayer, the Peace is exchanged.

If for some reason there is no celebration of the Holy Communion, the service concludes with the Lord's Prayer and such devotions as the bishop may direct.

The Celebration of the Holy Communion

The service continues with the Prayers of the People or the Offertory, the Confession being omitted. At the Offertory, the newly confirmed should present the bread and wine. Chrism may be consecrated after the post-communion prayer. The consecration of chrism may be prefaced by the address found in *The Book of Occasional Services*; music is found in *The Altar Book*.

A Form of Commitment
To Christian Service

This form is meant to be used at the Eucharist for those who wish "to make or renew a commitment to the service of Christ in the world, either in general terms, or upon taking some special responsibility." This is not intended as a form for admitting persons to parochial offices or ministries (for which *The Book of Occasional Services* provides a form), but for the service of Christ in the world, for the church's outreach. It might be appropriate:

    1. for those who have come to a renewed sense of Christian commitment—an alternative to the episcopal form for Reaffirmation for such persons;

    2. for those undertaking some form of community service out of a sense of Christian vocation;

3. for those going out on an assignment elsewhere with a service organization—the Peace Corps, Volunteers for Mission, Project Hope, or a similar organization.

It is set in the context of the ordinary Eucharist. The rubrics are somewhat unclear, but the order after the Gospel (and sermon) would seem to be as follows:

1. Renewal of Baptismal Vows, introduced by a specially drafted bidding, inviting the people to join with the person(s) making a special commitment in renewing the Baptismal Covenant;

2. The Prayers of the People, with special petitions for the person(s) making a special commitment;

3. The Act of Commitment, made before the congregation by the person(s) in the form either of a statement of intention or a series of questions and answers;

4. The celebrant's prayer for guidance and strength from the Holy Spirit for the person(s) and a commendation of the person(s) to the work on behalf of the congregation (a handshake would be an appropriate gesture here);

5. A prayer of blessing, to which a prayer for the work undertaken may be added (the people standing and the person[s] making the commitment kneeling).

6. The Peace and the remainder of the service.

The difficulty with this order is that if the Renewal of Baptismal Vows follows the Gospel (and sermon) as customary, the Prayers of the People must be intruded between them and the Act of Commitment. The order flows much more smoothly if the Prayers of the People are placed following the Peace, as in the baptismal liturgy.

The form of the Act of Commitment (number 3 above) should be carefully worked out ahead of time by the celebrant and the persons involved.

Commissioning for Lay Ministries in the Church

(The Book of Occasional Services)

This commissioning is intended for use after the homily (and Creed) at the Eucharist or at the time of the anthem or hymn after the prayer for mission at Morning Prayer or Evening Prayer. It may also be used separately. Special forms are provided for all the usual parish offices and ministries, as well as a general form.

The order of service for this rite, which would take place with the candidates and sponsors standing before the celebrant, is as follows:

1. The congregation is seated and the celebrant, sponsors, and candidates stand for the Presentation and Examination.

2. A scripture reading follows when the commissioning is used as a separate service.

3. For each candidate or group of candidates the appropriate form of admission is used. Each form includes a) a presentation sentence; b) antiphon, versicle, response, and collect; and c) a commissioning sentence. An appropriate token of the responsibility undertaken may be given at the commission, and a handshake is appropriate during the sentence.

4. A collect is given to conclude the Prayers of the People (when the form is used at the Eucharist) or to be used with the Peace to conclude the Office or to be used with the Lord's Prayer, Peace, and Blessing when the form is used as a separate service.

The antiphon, versicle, response, and collect might be set to the traditional tones to be sung, if desired. Other parts of the Office are better said.

The Celebration and Blessing of a Marriage

In *The Book of Common Prayer* 1979, the marriage service is set in the context of the Holy Eucharist. A special entrance rite is provided, the marriage itself is set between the Ministry of the Word (for which propers are provided) and a special form of the Prayers of the People which introduces the Blessing of the Marriage, and a proper preface and proper post-communion prayer are given. The celebrant under normal circumstances is a bishop or presbyter, since they alone are authorized to give the nuptial blessing and preside at the Celebration of the Holy Communion. A deacon or assisting presbyter may preside at the portion of the rite which precedes the Ministry of the Word and read the Gospel and assist in other ways. Lay persons should read the lessons before the Gospel. A deacon, lay person, assisting presbyter, or the celebrant may lead the prayers that precede the nuptial blessing. If civil law permits, a deacon may perform marriages when no bishop or presbyter is available, omitting the portions of the rite restricted to bishops and presbyters.

Preparations

The Canons require thirty days' notice before a wedding under normal circumstances. The celebrant should meet with the couple to instruct them on Christian marriage and to plan the service with them. The declaration must be signed. A parish is well advised to have a set of written policies on marriages to avoid disputes over music, flowers and decorations in the church, use of the parish facilities, fees, photography, and similar matters.

The usual color for hangings and vestments for weddings is white, although in Lent the Lenten array may remain in place. Seating should be planned for the wedding party. If the parish does not use an altar rail, a kneeler will need to be put in place for the nuptial blessing. A runner for the center aisle at weddings is common, though it serves no real purpose. If the couple want it, their florist should provide it. A printed program will greatly facilitate participation in the service, particularly when wedding guests may be unfamiliar with the Episcopal Church and its customs.

A rehearsal with participants and the organist should be planned for all but the smallest and most informal of weddings. The minister should require the couple to present their marriage license at that time, and it is appropriate for them and their witnesses to sign the register and necessary papers then also (this may be done in the course of the service, as the English do, but a signing during the service can be awkward). It is perhaps easiest to rehearse all the processions first, so that the organist can leave. Then the celebrant walks through the service in outline form with all involved. Those reading the lessons should rehearse their readings at this time. The ushers need to be given instructions about seating, location of restrooms, and similar matters.

The Entrance

The entrance processions as well as the final procession at weddings are matters of custom and tradition rather than rubrical requirement. Instrumental music is most common at the entrance, but a hymn, psalm, or anthem may be used. Customarily, the groom and best man enter with the celebrant and then await the rest of the wedding party which comes down the center aisle, the bride (and her escort) walking at the end of the procession. Variations in the order of procession are possible, depending on the layout of the church and the wishes of the bride and groom. Use of incense, cross, and torches in the procession(s) is possible, though probably of dubious significance in the bridal procession. For a very small wedding, the entire wedding party may simply come forward from the front pew as the celebrant enters. The congregation rises as the procession(s) enter.

At the end of the procession, the bride and groom stand before the celebrant, their attendants at their sides. This part of the rite usually takes place before the chancel step. The person(s) presenting the bride (and groom) would stand behind them. It is customary to stand throughout the entire wedding service (except for the lessons and homily), but the celebrant may instruct the congregation to sit at other times in the interest of visibility.

The opening exhortation is addressed to the congregation and the charge to the bride and groom. The declaration of consent follows. The celebrant should make certain that the congregation is cued in to make its response when asked to support the couple. At this point the bride (and groom) may be "presented." The bride's father, or parents, or a family member may present the bride; or both sets of parents may present the couple. The form to be used for the presentation is found on page 437. It is preferable to avoid using the word "give"; the bride is given neither as property nor as a person needing protection. At this point the bride's veil may be lifted. A hymn, psalm, or anthem may follow.

The Ministry of the Word

The celebrant says or sings (to a monotone or one of the collect tones) the collect. The congregation may then be seated for the readings before the Gospel. The wedding party may be seated also, or may continue to stand through the Ministry of the Word. A wide selection of Old Testament readings, epistles, and gospels is provided. Psalms, hymns, and anthems may be used between the readings. Appropriate psalms are listed; they are set to plainsong for responsorial recitation in *Gradual Psalms*. At least one lesson must be read; at a Eucharist, a Gospel must be read. The full Ministry of the Word is appropriate. A brief homily and/or the Apostles' Creed may follow. The rubric provides for other responses to the readings besides a homily. The celebrant should use caution here: selections from other literature or ceremonies or music that the bride and groom often desire have little relation to, and may be inconsistent with, a Christian understanding of marriage.

The Marriage

The bride and groom (and as many of their wedding party as space allows) may approach the altar now, or later before the nuptial blessing. A hymn, psalm, anthem, or instrumental music is appropriate during such a procession, although the rubrics make no explicit provision for it. The bride and groom should face each other as they make their vows. The bride will give her bouquet to an attendant before the vows. The vows should be prompted, a few words at a time, by the celebrant, or read from a book. It is better not to rely on memory at such a time. Ring(s) may be placed on the celebrant's book for blessing; they may be blessed here, or the celebrant may go to the altar for the blessing. The form for the exchange of ring(s) is also prompted by the celebrant a few words at a time. The non-trinitarian option respects the conscience of a bride or groom who may come from another faith. The celebrant may hold up the joined hands of bride and groom when announcing the marriage. The custom of wrapping the hands with the celebrant's stole is probably best avoided. This somewhat arcane ceremony gives the impression that it is the celebrant, not God, who joins the couple. The celebrant's true function is to witness and bless the marriage.

The Prayers and the Blessing

All stand for the Prayers. The Lord's Prayer is omitted if the Celebration of the Holy Communion is to be part of the service. The prayers are led by the deacon or other person appointed. The petition for children is omitted when circumstances require. Other petitions may be omitted if there is to be no Celebration of the Holy Communion, but it would be better to use them in their entirety. The bride and groom then kneel. The celebrant uses one of the two prayers provided and concludes with the nuptial blessing (stretching out a hand, laying on a hand, or making the sign of the cross). The couple rise. The Peace is exchanged. The bride and groom may go into the congregation to exchange it with family and friends at this time, but greetings here should not be too prolonged. The service may conclude at this point with the final procession (usually in reverse order, the bride and groom going first). A hymn, psalm, anthem, or instrumental music may be used for this procession.

The Celebration of the Holy Communion

If communion is to follow, the bride and groom should present the bread and wine. If they have gone into the congregation to exchange the Peace, they may bring the bread and wine back as they return. They may stand before the altar for the Great Thanksgiving and receive communion first, then retire to the side while others receive. Opportunity must be given for the congregation to receive at a nuptial Eucharist. A proper preface is provided for the Great Thanksgiving. When communions have been completed, the bride and groom return to stand before the altar. A proper post-communion prayer follows. Notes on the final procession are found above.

Music

A parish should have, as noted above, written policies on music for weddings to minimize conflicts and misunderstandings. The liturgical index of the Hymnal suggests appropriate hymns. *The Altar Book* provides music for the proper preface, the lessons, and the Gospel. The collect and post-communion collect might be monotoned or sung to one of the collect tones. It would be possible to sing the prayers before the nuptial blessing to a monotone, the celebrant's prayer to a monotone or a collect tone, and the blessing to the blessing tone, but in most cases it is probably more appropriate—and more conducive to the people's participation—to say them.

The Blessing of a Civil Marriage

This rite is set within the framework of an ordinary Eucharist, using the collect and propers from the marriage service. The traditional wedding processions might still be used in this service, but it would seem to make more sense to omit them, the couple coming forward after the Gospel (and homily).

At this time, the celebrant addresses the couple briefly and secures their consent to the obligations of Christian marriage with a set of vows. The support of the congregation is asked, ring(s) are blessed on the hand(s), the couple's hands are joined, and the prayers and nuptial blessing from the marriage service follow. The service continues with the Peace and the Celebration of the Holy Communion, at which the couple presents the bread and wine and the proper preface and post-communion collect from the marriage may be used. With slight adaptations (the use of the regular propers and the addition of the usual Prayers of the People), this rite might be incorporated into the Sunday parish Eucharist.

An Order for Marriage

Like similar provisions for the Eucharist and Burial, this order provides an outline within which participants can draft their own service. The specific directions of the rubrics and the fixed form for the marriage vows are meant to ensure that the resulting service conforms to the Church's understanding of Christian marriage. The rubrics are also so framed as to allow use of the 1928 rite. Ceremonial directions for the full rite above would in general apply here as well. Careful planning is necessary if this order is used.

The Anniversary of a Marriage
(The Book of Occasional Services)

This service is intended to be set within the context of a Eucharist, either the Sunday parish Eucharist or a special celebration. A proper collect is provided for a special celebration, and propers from the marriage service may be used.

The couple come forward after the Gospel (and Sermon and Creed, if appointed). The celebrant briefly addresses the congregation. At the celebrant's bidding, the couple renew their vows and then say a thanksgiving together. The celebrant then blesses the couple, using the form provided (and, if desired, the outstretched hand or the sign of the cross). The service continues with the Peace, or—at the parish Eucharist—with the Prayers of the People. The couple may present the bread and wine at the Offertory. If there is no Celebration of the Holy Communion, the service concludes with the Lord's Prayer and the Peace. The service may be adapted for use "as an act of reconciliation."

The Blessing of a Pregnant Woman
(The Book of Occasional Services)

If desired, this prayer and set of benedictions may be used, either privately, or before the Peace at the Eucharist, or at the time of the hymn or anthem after the prayer for mission in the Daily Office.

Thanksgiving for the Birth or Adoption of a Child

This replaces the rites in earlier editions of *The Book of Common Prayer* for the "churching of women." It is, in fact, truer to the ancient rites, which provide prayers for use on the eighth and fortieth days after the birth of a child (on the precedent of the days when Jesus was named and presented in the temple in Luke's Gospel). On occasion, the rite might be used in the hospital or home; in other circumstances, it is particularly appropriate for use at the first parish Eucharist a family attends after the birth or adoption of a child. If the Office is read daily in a parish, it would also be appropriate at such a service on the day that mother and child return from the hospital or that the family returns with a child they have adopted. At the Eucharist, the form follows the Prayers of the People. At the Daily Office, it would come at the prayers following the hymn or anthem after the prayer for mission. When used separately, the shorter form of the Office may be begun with one of the two lessons listed on page 439. At a baptism, the shorter form—or appropriate prayers from it—would be appropriate after the Prayers of the People. In services at church, the family will come before the celebrant for this thanksgiving. At a home or hospital, people take places as convenient.

The longer form of the Office begins as follows:

1. An address relating to the birth of a child or an address, questions, and acts acknowledging the inauguration of the new relationship in the case of an adoption.

2. The act of thanksgiving—a bidding and the Magnificat, Psalm 116, or Psalm 23. Metrical forms of the Magnificat or Psalm 23 might be sung, if music is desired, or the canticle or psalm may be sung to plainsong, Anglican Chant, or some other chant form.

The longer form of the office continues, and the shorter form begins, in this way:

3. A prayer of thanksgiving for the gift of a child.

4. Other prayers, as desired or appropriate—for a safe delivery, for the parents, for an unbaptized child, and for a baptized child.

5. A blessing of the family, if desired, and then the Peace.

The prayers might be monotoned or sung to a collect tone; the blessing sung to the blessing tone in *The Altar Book*. It is probably more appropriate in most circumstances to say them, however.

The Reconciliation of a Penitent

The introduction to this rite skillfully sets forth the various forms of the church's ministry of reconciliation. This is the first American Prayer Book to provide a form for Reconciliation as a separate Office. The rubrics make the rite available to all who desire it: those who make confession a regular part of their rule of life, those who come on a particular occasion because of a troubled conscience, and the seriously ill for whom it is part of "setting their house in order."

Confessions may, in case of necessity, be heard anywhere. Normally it is preferable that they be heard in church. "Confessionals" are probably best avoided, but the "reconciliation rooms" now designed for Roman Catholic churches are an ideal setting, and might be considered in parishes where there is frequent use of this pastoral rite. In most parishes, however, it will be best for the confessor to sit for the rite near the altar, or in a chapel which provides greater privacy. The confessor would sit in a chair by an altar rail or (if there is no rail) a chair by a prayer desk. Another chair may be provided for the penitent, following the provision of the rubrics that "confessor and penitent may sit face to face." The confessor might wear a stole over an alb (or over cassock and surplice).

In cases of necessity, a deacon or lay person may be asked to hear a confession. Absolution may be given only by a bishop or presbyter; a deacon or lay person uses a "declaration of forgiveness" in place of the absolution. This provision for deacons or lay persons as confessors is not an innovation, but a long-standing tradition in the church. The secrecy of a confession is absolute.

The first form of confession is that which will probably be used by those who make their confession regularly. The second by its wording is more appropriate for use by someone returning to the practice of the Christian faith after a long lapse, or to one seeking reconciliation after particularly serious sin; in any case, its tone makes it seem inappropriate for frequent use by a penitent.

The outline of Form One is as follows:

1. Request and blessing.

2. Confession.

3. Counsel, direction, and comfort.

4. Absolution (two alternative forms).

5. Dismissal

For Form Two, this would be the outline:

1. Verses from Psalm 51 with the Trisagion.

2. Request and blessing.

3. Scriptural words of comfort (sensitivity should be shown to inclusive language in selecting verses).

4. Invitation and confession.

5. Promise of repentance and willingness to forgive.

6. Absolution (two alternative forms).

7. Dismissal.

The confession here is partially cast in the framework of the parable of the prodigal son and is Eastern Orthodox, rather than Western, in its tone.

In both forms the confessor may make the sign of the cross over the penitent in the initial blessing and again at the absolution. In the second form, the gesture suggested by the rubrics at the absolution is the laying on of a hand or the outstretched hand: this may be used also with the first form. The Western formula of absolution is the first alternative in Form One; a formula in the Eastern style is the first alternative in Form Two. A declaration of forgiveness for use by a deacon or lay confessor is provided for use with each form. A sign of penitence or an act of thanksgiving may be assigned by the confessor, but it is not to be understood as a way of "earning" God's forgiveness: It is not a "penance" in the theological sense that the term has been used in the Roman Catholic theology of the rite in the past.

Ministration to the Sick

The provisions of *The Book of Common Prayer* 1979 for ministration to the sick begin with an initial greeting and are divided into three component parts:

1. *The Ministry of the Word:* sets of Epistle, psalm, and Gospel are provided under the headings "General," "Penitence," "When Anointing is to follow," and "When Communion is to follow." Other passages may be read, appropriate comments made, and prayers offered. The Reconciliation of a Penitent may follow, or a general confession and absolution.

2. *The Laying on of Hands and Anointing:* Oil for Anointing the Sick may be blessed. An anthem (printed as a versicle and response) is then said. Two forms are provided for the laying on of hands, and a form (in a shorter and a longer version) to be used for anointing. The Lord's Prayer is said, if it will not be used at Communion. A bishop or presbyter concludes with a prayer of blessing. The acts are restricted to a bishop or presbyter, though in cases of necessity, a deacon or lay person may anoint with oil blessed by a bishop or presbyter.

3. *Holy Communion* is administered from the Reserved Sacrament, or from a celebration beginning at the Offertory. A proper post-communion prayer is provided.

These provisions are all collected, with texts printed out in full, along with other related materials from the Prayer Book, in *Ministry to the Sick,* published by the Church Hymnal Corporation. This is a useful book for use with pastoral visitation of the sick.

Circumstances will determine which of the parts will be used on a particular occasion; but whatever parts are used follow the sequence given above. The order is intended primarily for use in pastoral ministrations with individuals outside of the church building, though it might be used with groups gathered for worship in a nursing home or similar institution. For a service intended for the sick in the parish setting, the provision of *The Book of Occasional Services* for a public service (see below) would ordinarily be used. These very flexible provisions are meant to be adapted to a variety of circumstances; the style of worship will be more informal and relaxed than would be customary or appropriate for a parish service. In most cases, vestments would not be worn, although they might be appropriate in the context of a service for a group gathered in a nursing home. A minister taking the sacrament from a public service in the church a short distance might remain in alb and stole or cassock, surplice, and stole. For sacramental ministrations, some may prefer to wear a stole over street clothes; others will prefer not to don a stole.

In the Ministry of the Word, circumstances will determine whether a full or abbreviated set of lessons will be used, and which set of propers is appropriate. If the person visited is housebound but not seriously ill, and if regular visitations are made, it may be appropriate to use the Sunday propers rather than those listed here; the proper collect might also be prefaced to the lessons. The psalm may also be read as a "lesson," rather than said in unison or responsively— particularly if it is difficult for the person visited to read or to participate actively in the service.

The prayers used after the lessons will also vary according to the situation. They might be appropriate prayers from this section of the Prayer Book, or a set of biddings by the minister (and the person visited) concluded by a general collect, or (in services for groups in nursing homes) a form of intercession from the Prayers of the People with a common response or a series of collects selected to follow the set topics of intercession. In many cases, active participation by the person(s) visited will be difficult, and this must be taken into account in choosing the prayers to be used here.

In some circumstances, the rite for the reconciliation of a penitent might best be used next—in which case others might be asked to leave the room for this part of the visitation. In other circumstances, a familiar form of the general confession will be used.

The Laying on of Hands and Anointing are the Church's sacramental ministry of healing. In the Middle Ages, these rites were generally understood as "last rites," and so were lost to the Church for its healing ministry. They were recovered for the Episcopal Church in the 1928 Prayer Book and have gradually become common once more in the life of the church. Caution is advisable in the use of these rites with older persons, however, lest they be understood in the mediaeval sense and frighten the person visited. In our present book, this part begins with a prayer for blessing oil for unction (an act restricted to bishops and presbyters). The anthem which follows is printed for use as a versicle and response. Two formulas are given for the laying on of hands, and a shorter and longer form for use in unction. If there is to be no communion, the Lord's Prayer follows. This part of the rite concludes with a prayer of blessing (which is restricted to bishops and presbyters). If used with sensitivity, the rite should leave the sick open to God's future: ready to accept healing and ready to face release from suffering through death.

Holy Communion is the last part of the rite for ministration to the sick. It may begin with the Peace. Normally, it is theologically preferable to administer communion from the Reserved Sacrament, which links the sick person to the worship of the congregation through the elements consecrated at the parish Eucharist. For those confined to home or an institution by long illness, it may be appropriate to use a full celebration at times. For communion from the Reserved Sacrament, the form is taken from the rite for Communion under Special Circumstances, beginning at the Lord's Prayer. A celebration may follow any authorized rite, beginning at the Offertory. In either case, vessels may be laid out on a table on a napkin or cloth available in the home, or linens may be brought from the church. For a celebration, vessels of sufficient size should be used in order not to trivialize the rite.

On some occasions, the minister might bring other friends and parishioners to join in the service. Some of them might read lessons and lead responses. The rite should be relaxed but structured. Circumstances will suggest what postures participants take. Large-print forms of the service are useful in ministering to those whose vision may be limited. It is important to use familiar forms for the same reason. As we have noted, a service in such situations may be much less participatory than is customary for public services in the parish. The energies of the sick should not be taxed by an effort to participate in unfamiliar forms of worship.

The normal celebrant of these rites is a bishop or presbyter. When necessity requires, Parts I and II may be led by a deacon or lay person, who would make the substitutions given in the rubrics for the absolution after the confession and would use oil blessed by a bishop or priest for unction. The rubrics make no provision for a deacon or lay person to administer the laying on of hands. A deacon may administer communion from the Reserved Sacrament using the form provided for Communion under Special Circumstances; a lay eucharistic minister may administer communion only after a parish celebration, and (at present) only with the form for this issued by the Standing Liturgical Commission.

Music would not ordinarily be used with these rites. It might be appropriate, in some situations, to sing hymns—particularly in a service for a group at a nursing home or similar institution.

A Public Service of Healing
(The Book of Occasional Services)

This service is set within the framework of the Holy Eucharist.

The Entrance

The ordinary entrance rite may be used, or the Penitential Order, or the greeting (and collect) printed in the text of this rite. In the latter case, this might presumably be preceded by a hymn, psalm, or anthem. A collect is given, or the collect of the day or some other suitable collect may be used.

The Ministry of the Word

A list of appropriate lessons is given, for use if the proper of the day is not used. As usual, a psalm, hymn, or anthem may be used between readings. Suitable psalms may be found in the *Gradual Psalms*; suitable hymns are listed in the liturgical index in the Hymnal.

The Prayers of the People

The Book of Occasional Services provides a Litany of Healing, which may be used for the Prayers of the People. It might be set to a tone for a litany and suffrages. The Litany of Healing may be introduced by the celebrant with an invitation to the congregation to name those for whom they wish to pray. Three options are provided for the concluding collect, or another collect may be chosen. A form of General Confession follows, if the service has not begun with the penitential order.

The Laying on of Hands and Anointing

Oil for unction may be blessed, using the form from the Prayer Book. The anthem from the Prayer Book rite (printed as a versicle and response) follows. Then those who wish to do so come forward for the laying on of hands (and anointing). The prayer of blessing from the Prayer Book rite follows. Three formulas are given for the laying on of hands; each may be expanded to include unction as well. Prayer may also be offered during the laying on of hands according to each person's need. Lay persons with the gift of healing may join in the laying on of hands.

A special issue arises from the not uncommon custom of coming forward to receive the laying on of hands or anointing on behalf of another. This healing "by proxy" borders on magic and is not theologically sound. It might be dealt with by having such persons come forward separately and using a prayer such as the following while hands are laid on:

> *God empower you by the might of the Holy Spirit, that you may be an instrument of the healing love of Christ in the lives of others (or in the life of _____).*

This conforms the language of the prayer to what is actually taking place. Such persons should not, however, be anointed; the oil of unction is specifically intended for healing the sick, not for strengthening others to minister to them. The service continues with the Peace. It may conclude at this point with the prayer and the blessing given at the end of the rite in *The Book of Occasional Services.*

The Celebration of the Holy Communion

If the Celebration of the Holy Communion is to be observed, the Offertory follows the peace. The prayer printed at the end of the rite is then used for the post-communion, followed by the blessing.

Ministration at the Time of Death

A variety of materials is provided by the Prayer Book for use with persons at or near the point of death and with those gathered with them. They are intended primarily for use by the Minister of the Congregation, who should be called at such a time, but they may be led by anyone in cases of necessity.

The first prayer is for a person near the point of death.

The Litany at the Time of Death is meant for use by those gathered round the dying person. It can also be used at a vigil before the burial or at a Rite II Burial Office. It is followed by two prayers of commendation and the final brief prayer for rest in peace.

Provision is made for a vigil held by friends and family before the burial. It might be held at the church, at a home, or at a funeral home. It is suggested that psalms, lessons, and collects from the burial office be used. For the prayers, the Litany at the Time of Death may be used, or a responsory printed on pages 465–466. An order of service for use at such vigils might be printed up by a parish. A vigil ought to provide both an opportunity for prayer and also a time to visit with the family and offer sympathy and support. It is best if two separate places be used for these two purposes—perhaps the church or a chapel for prayers, and the parish hall for the ministry of sympathy and hospitality. In church, the officiant might vest; elsewhere the service might be more informal in nature.

The Reception of the Body

Biddings and prayers are provided for use when a body is brought to the church—either for a vigil before the burial service, or immediately before the burial service is to begin. At such a time, the coffin is covered with the pall and may be led into church by a person carrying the lighted Paschal Candle.

The Burial of the Dead

This service, set in the context of the Holy Eucharist, is printed in both traditional language (Rite I) and contemporary language (Rite II). Both rites have the same basic structure, and we will consider them together. It should be noted that this service presents more problems with inclusive language than any other service of the Prayer Book, and considerable sensitivity is called for in this regard.

A parish would be well advised to print up forms for planning the burial office. This is useful both for those who wish to file funeral requests and for those who put together a service with the family when no requests have been filed. It can also set forth parish standards in regard to the use of the pall and the closed coffin, the use of flowers, and other matters.

Preparations

Choice of psalms, lessons, music, eucharistic prayer, and other details of a service should be worked out with the family by the Minister of the Congregation. A planning form, as noted above, is useful for this purpose. The services of the Prayer Book are flexible enough that the service can be tailored to each individual situation.

The rubrics of the Prayer Book state: "Baptized Christians are properly buried from the Church." Every effort should be made to encourage the use of the parish church (rather than a funeral home) for this service, and even for the vigil and wake. Every effort should also be made to schedule the service at "a time when the congregation has opportunity to be present." This may mean at times scheduling the service in the church after the committal rather than before it—perhaps an afternoon committal and an evening service in the church. If possible, opportunity should be given for the congregation to extend their sympathy to the bereaved, and parish facilities should be made available for this purpose. Such an opportunity might be given either after the burial office or at a vigil or wake.

The relation of the theology of this service to the resurrection means that the preferred color for hangings (including the pall) and vestments is white, although black and purple were frequently in use in earlier ages. The Paschal Candle stand should be set at the head of the coffin, beside the table with the urn of ashes, or (when the body or ashes are not present) in or near the chancel in the place customary during Easter Season. The candle itself will be used in the entrance procession, and it may also be used in the procession from the church (outside, however, a cross might replace it: it will be hard to keep lit outdoors). A coffin should be closed and covered with a pall (though the use of a flag may be permitted). A chalice veil may be used to cover an urn of ashes, which might be placed on a table in the place where the coffin usually stands (*not on the altar*). Flowers should be restricted by parish policy. Flowers are appropriate in the places customary at the parish Eucharist; some arrangements might be allowed in the narthex or parish hall; a spray may be used to cover the coffin when it is carried from the church (but it should not be used over or in place of the pall in the church). The ministers may wear the vestments customary for the eucharist, if there is to be communion; otherwise a stole is appropriate with alb (or cassock and surplice). Except for the special features of the rite, the ceremonial would be that of the parish Eucharist.

Pews should be reserved for family and pallbearers; a place might also be provided for these persons to gather before the service. A printed program will help those who are not familiar with Episcopal worship follow the service; the note on page 507 might be printed also.

Music

Hymns, psalms, and other music should express both the joy and certainty of the Christian hope of the resurrection and the grief and sorrow of bereavement. A false note is struck if either of these elements is avoided in music or in the texts of the rite. Easter hymns, All Saints' hymns, metrical psalms, and general hymns are all appropriate. Suitable hymns are listed in the liturgical index in the Hymnal. The psalms appointed may be sung to the settings in *Gradual Psalms,* to a plainsong psalm tone, to an Anglican Chant or Simplified Anglican Chant tune, or to one of the tones in the *Lutheran Book of Worship.* Metrical settings, when available, may also be used.

None of the forms of the Prayers of the People in this rite is set to music in the Hymnal (though the Litany at the Time of Death, which may be used with Rite II, might be set to the tones for the Great Litany and suffrages). Other forms might be monotoned. Collects and lessons may be sung to the customary tunes (though this might restrict the choice of readers).

The Hymnal does provide settings in the Service Music section for the entrance anthems of Rite I (S 375–387) and Rite II (S 380–382), the commendation anthem (S 383 for Rite II and also Hymn 355), and the anthems for the final procession (S 384–388 and also Hymn 354 and 356 [In Paradisum]). The second of the committal anthems for Rite I has a setting (S 379) as does the committal anthem of Rite II (S 389). A metrical setting of the commendation anthem is found as Hymn 358.

Participants

The proper celebrant at a burial is the Minister of the Congregation. The standard service is set in the context of a Eucharist, at which a bishop or presbyter must preside. In cases of necessity, a deacon or lay person may preside as celebrant, but there will be no Eucharist in this case. A deacon may lead the Prayers of the People, read the Gospel, and perform other functions customary at the Eucharist. Assisting presbyters may concelebrate and assist with communion and might take some other parts of the service assigned to the celebrant. Lay persons should read the lessons before the Gospel and may lead the Prayers of the People. The celebrant, in planning the service, should be sensitive to which family members or friends might read lessons. It is sometimes difficult emotionally for someone close to the person who has died to read in this setting, and it is important to avoid putting undue emotional strain on people at such times. The family or friends might present the bread and wine at the Offertory.

The Entrance

The ministers enter while one or more of the entrance anthems are sung. In Rite II, a hymn, psalm, or some other suitable anthem may be sung in place of the anthems printed in the text of the rite. A hymn has frequently been sung during the procession before the entrance anthems, and while there is no rubrical provision for this, this practice works well in some situations. The ministers may also enter in silence and read the anthems from the place customary for the acclamation at the Eucharist. The coffin or urn may be borne in behind the ministers in the entrance procession, or either of them may be in place at the head of the center aisle before the service begins. Settings for the entrance anthems are noted above. Sensitivity to inclusive language might lead to the (rubrically permissible) omission of the first and third of the anthems. Unfortunately, this is musically difficult with the settings of the anthems for Rite II. The entrance procession should be led by the Paschal Candle, unless the coffin or urn is already in place (in which case the candle will be beside it already lit). Cross, torches, and incense may also be carried in the entrance procession.

A rubric in Rite II states:

> *When all are in place, the Celebrant may address the congregation, acknowledging briefly the purpose of their gathering, and bidding their prayers for the deceased and the bereaved.*

Such an introductory address should be brief and carefully prepared.

The salutation and collect(s) follow. Rite I provides one collect for the burial of an adult and another for the burial of a child. Rite II provides three alternatives for the burial of an adult, one for the burial of a child, and a collect which may be added for the bereaved. Collects should be said or sung at the same place customary at the parish Eucharist.

The Liturgy of the Word

One or more lessons are used. Appropriate selections from Old Testament, New Testament, and the Gospel of John are listed. Appropriate psalms are also listed for use between the readings, and in Rite I the text of these psalms is printed out from the 1928 Prayer Book (also from the King James Bible for Psalm 23). If communion is to be celebrated, a Gospel is always read. The normative usage would be the three lessons customary at the Eucharist, but the scope of the rubrics allows for fewer (or more) readings. The readings would be announced and concluded as at the Eucharist, and the same ceremonial is appropriate. The rubrics regarding the use of psalms, hymns, and canticles between the lessons vary in wording. A hymn would not seem to be provided for after the Old Testament reading in Rite I (though a metrical psalm might be used). Note that in the burial Office the third option is a canticle, not an anthem. If psalms are read, it would seem best to read them in unison, although other methods of recitation are possible. Provisions for singing the psalms have been noted above. The Hymnal also provides settings for the canticles. In this rite, a full psalm is appropriate after the New Testament reading as well as after that from the Old Testament.

A homily may be preached by the celebrant in Rite I, by the celebrant or a friend or a relative in Rite II. It would also seem appropriate for an assisting minister to preach the homily. Note that it is to be a homily and not a eulogy. Its purpose is to draw out the way in which the lessons speak to the particular situation. Caution should be used if a relative or friend gives the homily: this may be emotionally difficult, and the person may find it hard to present a homily rather than a eulogy. The Apostles' Creed may follow. The bidding before the Creed in Rite II would also be appropriate in Rite I.

The Prayers

The prayers should be led from the same place as the Prayers of the People at the Eucharist, although the placement of the coffin or the urn at the head of the center aisle may require some adjustment in this position. If there is to be no communion, the Lord's Prayer precedes the other prayers, and either the prayers printed in the text of the rite or other suitable prayers (a selection of prayers is provided with each rite, for use here or at the committal) may be used. If other prayers are used, their number should be kept within bounds; one for the departed, one for the bereaved, and one for the congregation should suffice. The temptation to string together an endless series of collects should be resisted. A series of petitions is printed for the prayers in Rite I, with a doxology at the conclusion. The congregation joins in by replying to each petition with an Amen. In Rite II, a litany is provided with a common response and a concluding collect. The Rite I petitions (whose language might be adjusted) or the Litany at the Time of Death may also be used with Rite II.

If there is to be no Celebration of the Holy Communion, the service continues with the Commendation or the Committal, if the body or ashes are present, and the blessing and dismissal.

The Celebration of the Holy Communion

If the service continues with the Holy Communion, the Peace and the Offertory follow after the prayers. The family or friends may present the bread and wine at the Offertory. If the altar is to be censed at the Offertory, the coffin or urn may also be censed; however, this censing is better omitted and the coffin or urn censed at the commendation (see below). A proper preface and proper post-communion prayer are provided. The whole congregation is to be given opportunity to receive communion.

The Commendation

After the post-communion prayer (or after the prayers, if there is no communion) the ministers go to the coffin or urn for the commendation. An anthem with antiphon is provided for use at this time. The antiphon is the *proemion,* and the anthem the first *oikos,* of the Byzantine Kontakion of the Dead. The anthem may be said, the congregation joining in for the parts of the text in italics. It also may be sung to one of the settings provided in the Hymnal. The metrical version is useful for services when there is no choir. The rubric also permits some other anthem or hymn at this place. An appropriate choice might be the Nunc Dimittis or Psalm 23, if not used elsewhere in the service. If incense is used, the celebrant censes the coffin or urn at this time, walking around it. After the anthem, the celebrant says the prayer of commendation. An outstretched hand or the sign of the cross over the coffin or urn would be an appropriate gesture during this prayer. If for some reason there is to be no committal later, the committal office may replace the commendation. If the body is not present, neither commendation nor committal will be used.

The celebrant (if bishop or presbyter) may then bless the people, and the deacon or some other minister may dismiss them. Anthems are provided for use for the procession from the church; the Benedictus, Nunc Dimittis, and Pascha Nostrum are suggested as appropriate canticles for this procession; or a hymn may be sung. One of the anthems might also be used as an antiphon with a psalm (In Paradisum is traditionally paired with Psalm 114). If a hymn is sung in the church, the anthems or canticles may be said (or sung) as the procession goes from the church door to the grave or the hearse. The Procession may be led by the Paschal Candle and/or the cross. Torches and incense are also appropriate. At the door, the pall will be removed and a floral spray may be placed on the coffin. The celebrant may remove the chasuble at the door if it has been worn for the service and put on a cloak.

The Committal

If the cemetery is on church grounds or nearby, or if ashes are to be placed in a columbarium in the church or buried in a memorial garden on church grounds, the congregation may follow the ministers in procession to the place of committal. The procession may be led by the cross (a Paschal Candle will probably not stay lit outdoors), and lanterns and incense may also be used. The hymns and anthems suggested above, or appropriate psalms, may be used, with a choir if there is one to lead the singing. If the cemetery is some distance away, the ministers and others of the congregation will go by car.

At the gravesite or place of repose for the ashes, the anthems might be said or (if there is a choir) sung. Two alternative sets are provided for Rite I; one set for Rite II. If the committal is used when no burial office is to be celebrated at another time, the officiant may wish to add one or more lessons at this point in the service. If the grave is not on consecrated ground, a prayer is provided for the consecration of the grave. The ministers stand at the head of the grave or before the place where the ashes will be placed.

The prayer of committal is an adaptation of the Aaronic blessing. This is followed by the salutation and the Lord's Prayer. The celebrant may add such other prayers as are appropriate. Once again, an endless string of prayers should be avoided. A prayer for the departed, one for the bereaved, and one for the congregation should suffice. The traditional short responsive prayers for the departed may be added. A blessing for dismissal is given in both rites. In Rite II, the Easter acclamation with a dismissal is printed as an alternative.

Earth (not flowers) is cast on the coffin (or urn) during the prayer of committal, and the celebrant may extend a hand or make the sign of the cross. The grave might also be censed, if desired. The older custom was to fill in the grave before departing. That is not always possible now.

The prayers at the committal might be monotoned or sung to collect or blessing tones as appropriate; normally, it is probably better to say them. If there is to be no service at the church, the minister may wish to add one or more psalms and one or more readings before the prayer of committal.

An Order for Burial

This form, like similar forms for the Eucharist and for marriage, is basically an outline. Suitable texts may be selected to fill it in. It is for use "when, for pastoral considerations, neither of the burial rites in this book is deemed appropriate." It follows the same basic order as the printed burial rites, and the same ceremonial would be appropriate. The following are some of the situations in which it might be used:

1. When the use of the 1928 rite is requested.

2. When a specially composed Eucharistic Prayer is desired for Rite II.

3. When gender-specific language renders the other rites inappropriate.

4. When a rite is desired for one who did not profess the Christian faith. *The Book of Occasional Services* provides an anthem, a list of suitable psalms and readings, appropriate prayers, and a form for committal to be used with the order under such circumstances.

A service using this order should be carefully prepared.

CHAPTER 8

Episcopal Services

The section of the Prayer Book entitled "Episcopal Services" contains some services at which a bishop must preside (Ordinations, the Dedication and Consecration of a Church or Chapel) and one (The Celebration of a New Ministry) at which a bishop normally presides, although the bishop may if necessary appoint a deputy. *The Book of Occasional Services* lists as "Episcopal Services" various rites at which a bishop must preside (the Consecration of Chrism, Reaffirmation of Ordination Vows, the Recognition and Investiture of a Diocesan Bishop, the Welcoming and Seating of a Bishop in the Cathedral, and Setting Apart for a Special Vocation); others which may be delegated are found listed under Pastoral Services (Dedication of Church Furnishings and Ornaments, Founding of a Church, Restoring of Things Profaned, Secularizing a Consecrated Building).

Ordination

All the rites of Ordination have a similar structure: Ordinations are performed in the context of a Eucharist, in which the newly ordained then perform the functions appropriate to their order. The outline of the rites is as follows:

1. Entrance, Acclamation, Collect for Purity;

2. The Presentation of the Candidate(s);

3. The Litany for Ordinations or some other approved litany with the collect for Ordinations and/or the collect for the day;

4. The Ministry of the Word;

5. The Examination;

6. The Consecration of the Ordinand(s);

7. The Celebration of the Holy Communion, in which the newly ordained perform the functions of their order, with a special postcommunion prayer and provision for newly ordained bishops or presbyters to give the blessing, and newly ordained deacons to give the dismissal.

Candidates for ordination are presented in baptismal garb (alb, surplice, or rochet): by this rubric the Prayer Book declares that it is baptismal status (not prior ordination to another order) that is the basic requirement for ordination. The image of the church's ministry thus presented is one of separate and distinct orders of ministry, not one of a hierarchical ladder of orders. In this, the Prayer Book more accurately sets forth the biblical and patristic understanding of the church's ministry than the canons do, for they require prior ordination as deacon for presbyters and prior ordination as presbyter for bishops.

Participants

Christian worship is the "epiphany" of the church, the setting in which the functions of the various orders are revealed. This is especially true at ordinations, and the rubrics outline the functions of each order very carefully and very specifically. The functions specified for each order by the rubrics are as follows:

The Presiding Bishop (at the ordination of a bishop)
or the Bishop Ordaining (at other ordinations)

says the opening acclamation and collect
    (at the ordination of a bishop this may be delegated to another bishop)
presides at the Presentation
reads the collect after the litany
is the chief ordainer, reciting the consecration
initiates the Peace at the ordination of a deacon
is the principal celebrant
    (except at the ordination of a bishop)
leads the post-communion collect
    (at the ordination of a bishop this may be delegated to another bishop)
blesses the people (at the ordination of a deacon)

Bishop(s)

may say the opening acclamation and collect
    (at the ordination of a bishop)
may take part in the examination of a bishop-elect
lay hands on the bishop-elect in ordination
stand as concelebrants at the altar
may lead the post-communion collect
    (at the ordination of a bishop)

A newly ordained Bishop

initiates the Peace
is principal celebrant at the Eucharist
blesses the people

Presbyter(s)

act as presenters of candidates for ordination
may lead the litany
read the Gospel in the absence of a deacon
join in the laying on of hands
    (at the ordination of a presbyter)
may prepare the altar in the absence of deacons
stand as concelebrants at the altar
at the fraction may prepare elements for
    distribution in the absence of a deacon

may perform ablutions in the absence of a deacon
may give the dismissal in the absence of a deacon

A newly ordained Presbyter

initiates the Peace
concelebrates the Eucharist
may be asked to give the blessing

Deacon(s)

may lead the litany (their traditional function)
read the Gospel
prepare the altar at the Offertory
at the fraction prepare elements for distribution
perform the ablutions
give the dismissal
may take the sacrament to the absent

A newly ordained Deacon

performs the diaconal functions above

Lay persons

act as presenters of candidates for ordination
may lead the litany
read the lessons before the Gospel
present the bread and wine
    (as family and friends of the ordinand)

In reflecting on these directions, we see that functions proper to one order which circumstances may require assigning to another order in an ordinary Eucharist are definitively restricted to that order in ordination rites. The exception is the diaconal functions. Because the diaconate has long been a vestigial order, treated as a temporary apprenticeship for the presbyterate, deacons may in fact not be available at all ordinations. The rubrics do take this reality into account. There can be no ordination, however, without the presence of bishop, presbyters, and lay persons. With the restoration of the vocational diaconate as a functional order, deacons should be available to perform their proper functions at ordinations in the years to come.

Vestments

Candidates for ordination are presented in baptismal garb (alb, surplice, or, in the case of candidates for the episcopate, rochet); no stole or symbol of order or academic honor is to be worn. Candidates are then clothed in the vestments appropriate to their order after ordination. Full vestments in Western tradition in the contemporary situation would be alb, stole, chasuble, and miter for bishops; alb, stole, and chasuble for newly ordained presbyters and concelebrating presbyters; alb (or cassock and surplice) and stole for other presbyters; and alb, deacon's stole, and dalmatic for deacons (the dalmatic is sometimes omitted at the present time, especially if the Byzantine form of the deacon's stole is used). Lay persons with specific functions in the service who are seated in the chancel might wear alb or cassock and surplice; they sometimes wear academic gowns and hoods, but (as with clergy) this usage is perhaps better avoided as being unrelated to their function in the service. The ordaining bishop might carry the pastoral staff; the primatial cross might be carried before (not by) the Presiding Bishop. Since the primatial cross and the pastoral staff are in origin quite distinct from each other, the Presiding Bishop may use both—carrying the staff and having the cross carried before him. Bishops might wear the cope in place of the chasuble (an Anglican variant of Western tradition), but it is preferable that they not change from cope to chasuble in the course of the service. In ordination, change of vesture signifies the new status of the newly ordained candidate; it is confusing to have the bishop change vesture as well.

Other vestments are possible. The range of options is set out in Chapter 1. It is preferable, however, that there be consistency in the vestments worn by the participants. The traditional liturgical color for ordinations is red or white; on a feast or Sunday, the color appropriate to the day might be worn.

Preparations

The rites of ordination are among the most complex in the Prayer Book and require careful planning. This is especially true of the ordination of a bishop, which may attract the largest congregation of all diocesan services.

The use of space should be carefully thought out in planning the service. The bishop's chair should be placed before the altar. In the ordination of a bishop, other bishops (or at least the two coconsecrators) are seated to the Presiding Bishop's left and right. Other bishops might be seated to the sides of the chancel. Seats for participating clergy are allotted on the chancel platform, if possible. Otherwise, places must be reserved for them at the front of the congregational seating. The candidate is seated in the congregational seating with presenters for the ministry of the word, and in the chancel after ordination. Lay participants come forward from the congregational seating or, if vested, are seated in the chancel.

Adequate communion stations (with open access) should be allowed for; there should be at least one station (staffed with one person administering the bread and one or two administering the cup) for every one to two hundred communicants. A stand should be available for signing the oath of conformity (otherwise someone must hold this on a book for signature by the candidate). A litany desk may be placed at the head of the center aisle for the litanist. Space should be provided to lay out the candidate's vestments and other symbols of office until the time of vesting after ordination. The Bible to be presented by the bishop should be close at hand for presentation when required or carried by a person who can unobtrusively hand it to the bishop when needed. Sufficient vessels for communion must be set on the credence or another convenient table. Large vessels may be required to consecrate adequate bread and wine. For the ordination of a bishop, where large numbers of people are to be communicated, a receiving basin for alms might serve as the paten and large flasks may be used to consecrate the wine.

Civic centers or auditoriums are often used these days for the ordination of a bishop. Careful thought is necessary in such services to make the best use of platform space (which serves as the chancel area) and to provide appropriate communion stations. The public address system needs to be considered too. Sight lines, audibility, and the accessibility of the communion stations are important considerations on such occasions.

Orders of procession need to be carefully planned. At the ordination of a bishop, where various groups and representatives of diocesan organizations may be in procession, it may be best to have several processions enter simultaneously and proceed down separate aisles.

The service leaflet should be carefully laid out to allow the congregation to follow the service easily. At services held in places other than a church, it is best to print out the entire service— otherwise adequate numbers of Hymnals and Prayer Books will need to be available for distribution. The leaflets should be carefully rubricated for participants, with clear and exact directions written in each participant's program. Rehearsals are useful, but they are not always possible when participants come from considerable distances. Processions and the orderly and efficient distribution of communion introduce enough complexity into the service; the ceremonial of the service itself should be kept functional and simple.

Entrance, Acclamation, Collect for Purity

The participants enter in procession and take their places. The rubrics provide for a hymn, psalm, or anthem during the entrance. It is also possible to enter during instrumental music. If large numbers enter in procession, it may prove best to begin the entrance to instrumental music and begin the hymn after the procession is well into the church. Because of the numbers involved in the ordination of a bishop, the options during the entrance in this service are all put in the plural. Careful planning, however, should keep the entrance from taking too much time even at the consecration of a bishop. Except at the ordination of a bishop, the ordaining bishop begins the service with the seasonally appropriate acclamation and the collect for purity. When a bishop is being ordained, the Presiding Bishop may delegate these functions, though it is liturgically preferable not to do so. The acclamation and collect may be sung to the customary tones if desired. The ordinand(s) and presenters may come and stand before the bishop ordaining after the entrance procession, or they may go to their seats and then come before the bishop after the collect for purity.

The Presentation of the Candidate(s)

The candidate(s) are then presented to the ordaining bishop by the presenters. The presenters then certify that the candidate(s) have been properly selected for ordination. At the ordination of a bishop, this takes the form of testimonials. Neither *The Book of Common Prayer* nor the Constitution and Canons cover the *exact* form of these testimonials. The customary forms, usually read by several persons, are unduly lengthy and sound more appropriate to a court of law than to a service of worship. It would be preferable to use a single brief form, similar to the one provided in the *Book of Occasional Services* for the Recognition and Investiture of a Diocesan Bishop. After this, the ordinand(s) take the oath of conformity. The ordaining bishop then asks for the consent and support of those present.

The Litany for Ordinations

The service continues with the Litany for Ordinations or some other approved litany, which the bishop ordaining then concludes with the salutation and collect. The litany is led by the person appointed. Traditionally, this would be a deacon; otherwise a lay person, presbyter, or even a bishop may lead this litany. The rubrics specify that all kneel for the litany, so a litany desk should be provided for the litanist. The ordinand and presenters customarily return to their seats in the congregation for this litany. In the Roman Rite, ordinands prostrate themselves during the litany, but this has not been the usual custom in the Anglican Rite. The concluding collect is either the

Collect of the Day or that for ordination, or both. It would be appropriate to use the collect of the day for a Sunday out of ordinary time or for a major feast. Music for the litany is found in the Appendix of the Hymnal at S 390. The collect may be sung to any of the ordinary tones.

The Ministry of the Word

Appropriate lessons are provided for ordination to each order. The lessons may, if desired, be sung to the customary tones. On major feasts and Sundays, the bishop ordaining may select one or more readings from the proper of the day. Ordinarily, lessons should be chosen in consultation with the preacher. The first two lessons *must* be read by lay persons. The Gospel *must* be read by a deacon, if one is present, at the ordination of deacons and presbyters, and *should* be read by a deacon at the ordination of a bishop. Otherwise, a presbyter reads the Gospel. If a significant part of the congregation or the diocese speaks a language other than English, a lay or ordained reader may also read the Gospel in that language. The Gradual Psalm follows the first lesson (*Gradual Psalms* and *The Psalmnary* provide responsorial settings, or it may be sung in other ways). A hymn, psalm, or anthem follows the Epistle; an alleluia verse may also be used, if desired. The sermon follows directly after the Gospel. Ordination sermons often conclude with a charge to the ordinand, who may be asked to rise for the charge. Except at the ordination of a bishop, the Nicene Creed follows the sermon. At the ordination of a bishop, a hymn follows at this point.

The Examination

The ordinand then comes before the Bishop ordaining, who continues with an address and examination. At the ordination of a bishop, the Presiding Bishop may delegate questions to one or more other bishops, and the bishop-elect ends the examination by leading the congregation in the Nicene Creed.

The Consecration

All stand except the ordinand(s), who kneel before the bishop ordaining. At the ordination of presbyter(s), the presbyters present gather to the right and left of the bishops ordaining; at the ordination of a bishop, the bishops present do so. The Veni Creator Spiritus or the Veni Sancte Spiritus is then sung. The rubric no longer requires that it be sung responsively, and there is no liturgical reason that it should be sung in this way.

The bishop ordaining then says or sings the prayer of consecration. The present Roman Rite sets this prayer to the preface tone; there is currently no published setting of the prayer in our rite. If there is more than one candidate, only the central portion of the prayer is repeated for each candidate. It is during this portion that hands are laid on by the bishop ordaining. At the ordination of a bishop, other bishops join in this act; in the ordination of a presbyter, the presbyters present do so. The bishop alone lays on hands to ordain a deacon. In the ordination of a bishop, the coconsecrating bishops also join in reciting the words of the central portion of the prayer.

The vesting of the newly ordained minister follows. Tradition will determine what vestments are used. Western tradition would specify stole (and dalmatic) for deacons; stole and chasuble for presbyters; and stole, chasuble (not cope), and miter for bishops. Then a bible is presented to the newly ordained; other symbols of office might also be presented. These might include a ring, cross, and pastoral staff for a bishop and a chalice and paten for a presbyter. The presenters or other persons may bring the vestments and symbols to the bishop ordaining to present and may assist in the vesting.

The rubrics specify that a new bishop be presented to the people at this point and suggest that applause is appropriate. The presentation and applause would be appropriate for newly ordained deacons and presbyters as well, though the rubrics do not specify it. The Peace is initiated by a newly ordained bishop or presbyter; at the ordination of deacon(s), by the bishop ordaining. The clergy present then greet the newly ordained, and after this family and others. A newly ordained bishop may be installed in the episcopal chair after this, if ordained in the cathedral church. A form for this may be found in *The Book of Occasional Services.*

The Celebration of the Holy Communion

Deacons, if present, prepare the table. This function is reserved for newly ordained deacons at their ordination. When the table is prepared, the concelebrants gather there for the Great Thanksgiving. The principal celebrant is the bishop ordaining, except at the ordination of a bishop, where the newly ordained bishop presides. Other (bishops and) presbyters stand at the table as concelebrants. Newly ordained presbyters always are among the concelebrants at their ordination Eucharist. A reasonable number of concelebrants should be selected to stand at the altar; other (bishops and) presbyters may stand in a semicircle behind those at the altar if space permits. At the fraction, deacons (or presbyters, if no deacons are present) bring vessels to the altar and divide the elements to distribute to those who will minister communion. Adequate communion stations should be planned, as noted above, for efficient administration of the sacrament: this is especially important at the ordination of a bishop. In practice, when there are large numbers administering communion, it proves easiest for the ministrants to communicate each other at their stations, rather than to receive at the altar before they go to their stations. Persons should be assigned to supply additional bread and wine as necessary to those administering communion.

After communion, the vessels and remaining elements should be taken to the sacristy for consumption and the ablutions. This is the function of deacons. It is especially appropriate that deacons or others be assigned to take the sacrament to those who could not be present for the service. The post-communion prayer should always be printed in the service leaflet with the name(s) of the person(s) ordained. It is led by the bishop ordaining; at the ordination of a bishop, the Presiding Bishop may delegate this to another bishop. It would be appropriate for the ordinand to kneel before the altar for this prayer. The blessing follows. A newly ordained bishop gives the episcopal blessing, for which a special form is provided and music is found at S 173 and in *The Altar Book*. The bishop ordaining may invite a newly ordained presbyter to give the blessing, using the form in that rite (music in *The Altar Book*). A deacon (or a presbyter if no deacon is present) gives the dismissal. This is done by a newly ordained deacon at the ordination of deacons.

The Additional Directions provide for a hymn of praise to be sung at this point at the ordination of a bishop. Traditionally, this hymn was the Te Deum. The final procession would precede the dismissal (except when the Te Deum or other hymn of praise is sung at the ordination of a bishop). Because of the number of those in procession, a hymn is appropriate during this procession, though there is no rubrical provision for it. Otherwise, instrumental music might be used.

The Reaffirmation of Ordination Vows
(The Book of Occasional Services)

This service is set in the context of a celebration of the Eucharist. It may be used:

    1. At a gathering of diocesan clergy during Holy Week (preferably before Maundy Thursday; in any case it is not to replace the proper liturgy of that day);

    2. At a clergy conference or some similar gathering of diocesan clergy with their bishop;

    3. When a presbyter celebrates an anniversary of ordination;

    4. When a presbyter is being received from another denomination whose orders are recognized by this church or is being restored to the ministry.

At diocesan gatherings which include deacons the reaffirmation of presbyteral vows may be preceded by reaffirmation of diaconal vows, introduced by an appropriate address. If only presbyters are present at such a gathering, however, such an addition to the rite would seem to reinforce a view of the ministry which does not take the three orders seriously as separate and distinct orders—a view which the ordination rites themselves (though not the canons) would seem to be seeking to avoid. When the service is used to receive a presbyter from another denomination or to restore a suspended or deposed presbyter, the oath of conformity is taken before the bishop's affirmation and the presbyter is greeted by the bishop at the Peace and vested as a presbyter at this point in the service.

A special collect is provided and lessons are suggested. The litany for ordinations may be used for the Prayers of the People. The bishop presides from a chair placed before the altar. The reaffirmation follows the sermon.

Oils for chrism and unction may be consecrated for diocesan use when this service is used at a gathering of diocesan clergy. The oils may be brought forward at the Offertory and placed on a table (not the altar). They are blessed by the bishop after the post-communion prayer, using the forms from *The Book of Common Prayer.* A special introduction for the consecration of chrism is provided by *The Book of Occasional Services,* and a similar one might be drafted for the blessing of the oil of unction. *The Book of Common Prayer* and *The Book of Occasional Services* make no provision for the use of the oil of catechumens; therefore there is no reason to bless it at such a service. A special proper is provided for use if desired when chrism is consecrated.

If oils are consecrated at such a service, provision should be made for distribution to diocesan clergy after the service. In such cases a supply of appropriate containers will need to be obtained as part of the preparation for this service. In addition, a supply of chrism should be kept reserved at the cathedral for distribution to clergy as needed at other times. Clergy who need oil of unction at other times may bless it themselves.

The Recognition and Investiture of a Diocesan Bishop

(**The Book of Occasional Services**)

This service, set in the context of a Eucharist, is meant for use when a bishop is translated to be diocesan in a new diocese, or when a bishop coadjutor succeeds to the office of diocesan bishop or a suffragan has been elected diocesan. The special features of the rite are *the Recognition* (which replaces the customary entrance rite), and *the Examination, the Investiture,* and *the Seating,* which follow the sermon. The Litany for Ordinations, with the collect for the day or the Collect for Ordinations, concludes the recognition. Various proper lessons are suggested. The diocesan is the chief celebrant at the Eucharist, which is concluded by a special post-communion prayer and the bishop's blessing. If the service is held outside the cathedral church, the seating will be omitted.

The ministers and people assemble before the rite begins. Since their entrance is not a part of the rite itself, the clergy, choirs, and others in the chancel enter unobtrusively, perhaps to the accompaniment of instrumental music. This entrance is a strictly functional procession, not a part of the rite itself. When all are in place, the Presiding Bishop is escorted to the chair placed before the altar. Then a welcoming procession of representative persons is formed and goes silently to the principal doors of the church. The bishop, attended by two deacons, stands outside the door and knocks three times to be admitted. The Warden (the President of the Standing Committee) opens the doors as an appropriate versicle and response are exchanged by the bishop and warden. The welcoming procession now escorts the bishop to the Presiding Bishop. Psalm 23 with an antiphon is suggested for this procession. The bishop petitions for recognition and investiture, the Presiding Bishop requests evidence of proper election (which is read) and the recognition and support of the people.

The Litany for Ordinations or some other litany is then sung or said. It is concluded by the Presiding Bishop by the Collect for the Day or the Collect for Ordination, and the service continues with the liturgy of the word. Various lessons are suggested. After the sermon and the Creed, an Examination follows, in which the bishop renews the commitments of ordination.

The bishop is now formally invested by the Presiding Bishop. A pastoral staff may be presented to the bishop by the former bishop or the Warden. The bishop now takes an oath to fulfill the responsibilities and obligations of the office, laying a hand on a Bible brought from the altar.

The Seating follows. The bishop is escorted to the cathedra; during this time instrumental music may be played. The Dean formally installs the bishop in the chair. Applause, acclamation, and a fanfare with bells or trumpets may follow. The Bishop then initiates the Peace. The Eucharist continues with the Offertory and concludes with a special post-communion prayer and the bishop's blessing.

Welcoming and Seating of a Bishop in the Cathedral
(The Book of Occasional Services)

The situation for which this rite is appropriate are set forth in the opening rubrics, along with notes on how the forms are to be used:

> *This service is intended for use when a new bishop has not been seated in the cathedra of the diocese at the time of ordination or at the time of recognition and investiture.*

> *Normally, it will take place on the occasion of the first visit of the bishop to the Cathedral.*

> *On a Sunday or other major Holy Day the Proper is that of the Day. On other days it may be one of those appointed for Various Occasions.*

> *If, however, the seating takes place shortly after the service of ordination or investiture held on the same day in a place other than the Cathedral, only the opening ceremonies of this service are used,*

concluding with the Te Deum or Gloria in excelsis with the Lord's Prayer, the bishop's blessing, and dismissal.

As in the service of Recognition and Investiture, the congregation and clergy gather before the service begins. The entrance of clergy and choirs should be an unobtrusive procession, probably to instrumental music. It is a preliminary to the rite, not part of the rite itself. As the rite begins, a procession consisting of the Dean, the Cathedral Clergy, the Cathedral Chapter, and other representative persons goes to the main doors of the cathedral. The Bishop (attended by two deacons) knocks at the door three times and they are opened by the person designated as Warden. The Bishop enters and greets the congregation. The procession then escorts the bishop to a place (probably the chancel) where the service will continue. This procession is accompanied by a psalm or anthem. The Dean's welcome, the Bishop's petition to be seated, and the seating follow. Instrumental music may be played as the bishop is escorted to the cathedra. After the seating, acclamations, applause, and a musical fanfare (with bells and/or trumpets) may follow. The Te Deum, Gloria in excelsis, or some other song of praise is now sung. The service then continues with the collect and the eucharistic liturgy, concluded by a special post-communion prayer and the episcopal blessing. As noted above, if the seating takes place on the same day as the ordination or investiture, there is no eucharistic liturgy and the service concludes with appropriate prayers and the blessing after the song of praise.

Celebration of a New Ministry

This particular rite provides for what we would customarily call the "installation" of a minister in a new position. In the early centuries of the church's life bishops, presbyters, and deacons customarily served the church that had presented them for ordination for life, so that there was no need for such a service. The chief minister at this service is the bishop; but the bishop may, if necessary, delegate this function to another person (presumably an ordained person, though the rubrics are not explicit on this matter). Each order of ministers performs its customary functions in this service, set in the context of a Eucharist. The bishop, if present, is the chief celebrant; otherwise the bishop's delegate presides until the Offertory, and the person being inducted, if a presbyter, is the chief celebrant.

The institution, with the litany for ordinations or some other appropriate litany, replaces the customary entrance rite and the prayers of the people. After the Liturgy of the Word the Induction precedes the Peace. At the Celebration of the Holy Communion, a special post-communion prayer is provided and the new minister, if a presbyter, may be invited by the bishop to give the blessing. The rubric allows the service to be adapted as circumstances require.

Preparations

The church is prepared as for a regular Eucharist. The bishop's (or institutor's) chair is placed in the midst of the chancel before the altar. The symbols of the new ministry might conveniently be placed on a table to the side or rear of the church (or at the front, provided that the view of chancel and altar is not obstructed) until they are presented. As at ordinations, seating, the order of procession, and communion stations should be thought out ahead of time. Service leaflets for participants should be individually rubricated.

The Institution

The procession enters during a hymn, psalm, or anthem and all take their places. The new minister is brought before the bishop or institutor by the wardens and/or other presenters. After the Presentation the bishop reads, or has another read, the official letter of institution. The new minister pledges commitment to the new ministry and the congregation pledge their support. The new minister and presenters then go to seats in the congregation. The litany follows, all kneeling or standing. The litany is concluded by the bishop or deputy with the salutation and collect in the text or the collect of the day. Music for the Litany for Ordinations is found at S 390; the collect may be sung to the customary tones.

The Liturgy of the Word

A selection of lessons and psalms is provided. Others from the
ordination of a deacon or Various Occasions may be substituted as
appropriate. Lessons, psalm, and Gospel may be sung in the
customary ways. The bishop, the new minister, or another person may
then give the sermon or an address. Responses may be made to the
address, if desired; if this is done, their length should be kept within
reason.

The Induction

A hymn follows the sermon. During this hymn the new minister goes
and stands beside the bishop, while those who will present symbols of
the new ministry go to the table where the symbols have been readied
and line up in the appropriate order. They should come forward with
one symbol at a time and then return to their places. A minister or
acolyte takes the symbols from the new minister and puts them in
appropriate places. The water should be presented in a ewer, not a
cruet: it is water for baptism. The new minister may wear only alb (or
cassock and surplice) until this part of the service, and put on stole
(and vestments) presented at the Offertory. The bread and wine
presented may be used at the Eucharist. Other symbols besides those
in the text may also be presented with appropriate words. After the
presentation the minister, if a presbyter, may be escorted to the chair
customarily assigned in the church and there, or in the midst of the
chancel, may kneel and say the prayer printed in the text. At the
bishop's invitation, the congregation greets the new minister (and
family). The new minister initiates the Peace.

The Celebration of the Holy Communion

At the Offertory, alms are collected and presented and a deacon or
other person appointed prepares the altar. The bishop and presbyters
gather at the altar for the Great Thanksgiving. The bishop, if present,
is the principal celebrant; otherwise a newly-instituted presbyter
presides at the celebration. The institutor leads the people in the

proper post-communion prayer. Then the new minister may be invited
to bless the people. The post-communion hymn may be sung as the
procession goes out, and a deacon (or presbyter in the absence of a
deacon) dismisses the congregation.

The Consecration of Chrism
Apart from Baptism
(The Book of Occasional Services)

Over the centuries it became customary to consecrate the oils needed
for use in initiation (oil of exorcism, also known as oil of the
catechumens, and oil of chrism) prior to the principal baptismal
liturgy of the year at Easter. Eventually Maundy Thursday became the
day fixed for this. Oil for unction of the sick also came to be blessed
at the same time. The new Prayer Book gives priority to a Baptism
over which a bishop presides in a parish as the preferred time for
blessing chrism and allows bishop or presbyter to bless oil for unction
in the context of rites for ministration to the sick. It makes no
provision for the oil of catechumens.

The Book of Occasional Services gives directions for consecration of
chrism at other times—at a parish Eucharist where the bishop
presides but does not administer Baptism and at a diocesan service.
Oil of unction might also be blessed on these occasions if desired. The
oil(s) may be presented at the Offertory, but they are to be placed on
some table other than the altar; they are then blessed after the post-
communion prayer. A brief address is given to introduce the
consecration of chrism. A similar one might be drafted to introduce
the blessing of the oil of unction.

If the bishop consecrates the oils for use throughout the diocese at a
special service, the special propers provided may be used. The
consecration of oils may also take place in the context of the
Reaffirmation of Ordination Vows as noted above.

The Founding of a Church

(The Book of Occasional Services)

The Groundbreaking

At groundbreaking the bishop, or a presbyter as the bishop's deputy, goes in procession with ministers and people to the site of the new building. The site is prepared before the service with four stakes at the corners, three cords (two for the diagonals and one for the circumference), and a spade at the place for the altar. During the procession a litany for the church is said or sung.

A hymn may follow. Then a lesson from Genesis is read and a sermon or address may follow. Two psalms with antiphons are given to be sung while the cords are stretched around the stakes on the diagonals and around the circumference. Then at the site of the altar the celebrant announces the dedication name and breaks the ground. The Lord's Prayer, versicles and responses, and a collect conclude the service.

Laying the Cornerstone

The following order is given for laying the cornerstone:

1. A hymn or anthem.

2. A reading from Scripture.

3. An address.

4. The collect of the patron or title, or some other appropriate collect.

5. The laying of the cornerstone, with a prayer and other texts.

6. A hymn, blessing, and dismissal.

If this takes place after the church is built, the ceremony occurs after the homily at a Eucharist. In this case, items 4–5 above are used.

The Dedication and Consecration of a Church

This is perhaps the most elaborate and complex service likely to be held in a parish church. Indeed, it is a service which many parishes will never have occasion to use. Unlike the service of prior Prayer Books, this one does not presuppose that the building be debt-free (though our canons have not caught up in this matter). The service in its entirety presupposes that this will be the *first* service in a new building—something which exigencies of the construction process and the bishop's schedule may sometimes make impossible.

Preparations

A place of assembly near the church—an outdoor site or the parish hall—should be readied for the initial gathering of people and officiants. If circumstances require, however, all but the bishop and other officiants may gather in the church.

The various appurtenances to be used in the new church may be carried in the procession or set out in the church to be put in place or put to use at the appropriate time. These might include:

For the font
a ewer of water, baptismal shell, linens, candles, and the Paschal Candle

For the lectern
the lectern Bible or lectionary texts, candles

For the pulpit (if distinct from the lectern)
the Gospel book, a pulpit fall

For the altar
frontal, fair linen, vessels, communion linens, candles, altar book and stand or cushion, and (for the credence table or shelf) lavabo bowl with towel and a cruet of water as well as a receiving basin for alms

For the oblations table or shelf
bread and wine, alms basins

Other items
flowers, book of remembrance, list of donors, property deed, blueprint, keys, tools used in construction, oils to be consecrated for chrism and unction, banners or hangings

Because of the complex nature of the service, it may be well to print the program out in full, at least through the Offertory. Texts and music to be used before the procession enters the church will in any case need to be printed out, since it is awkward to deal with books in procession.

The participants will include the bishop, the clergy of the parish, the wardens (and perhaps vestry and building committee), neighboring clergy, and acolytes. As noted above, the rest of the people also should be in the entrance procession if possible. Incense may be carried in the procession, and objects may be censed as they are dedicated.

Music

Special music may be sung in procession. The various forms of dedication might be set to music; on the whole it is probably better to say them, however. The customary parts of the Eucharist may be sung.

The Gathering

At the place of gathering, the bishop begins with an opening address and collect. Necessary announcements may be made at this time. The procession forms and approaches the main door of the church. During this procession instrumental music and singing are appropriate. The music should be relatively simple in nature or very well known to the people.

The Entrance and Consecration of the Church

The doors are opened and the bishop signs the threshold with the pastoral staff or processional cross and says the words of greeting. Hymns and anthems may be sung as the people take their seats and the officiants go to the place where the prayer for the consecration of the church will be said—probably near the entrance or at the front of the congregational seating. The prayer of consecration is divided into several portions, recited in turn by bishop, warden (or a representative of the congregation), and the minister of the congregation; the bishop concludes the prayer with the doxology, said responsively with the people. As the procession moves between stations, appropriate hymns, psalms, or anthems may be sung. The organ is not intended to be used until it is dedicated later in the service.

The Consecration of the Font

The procession moves to the font, which is dedicated with a prayer, a versicle and response, and a sentence of consecration (similar sets are used for lectern, pulpit, and musical instrument). Here and at other dedications, the bishop may stretch out the hand or make the sign of the cross during the prayer (and again at the sentence of dedication— although both text and gesture are really superfluous after the prayer). A Baptism may follow the consecration of the font: the baptismal Gospel and the rest of the rite from the presentation to the reception of the newly baptized is used. If there is no Baptism, water may be poured into the font and blessed with the form given in the text; the consecration of chrism may follow. Although the text of the rite does not provide for it, it might be appropriate to use the renewal of baptismal vows at this time if there has been no Baptism.

The Dedication of Lectern, Pulpit, and an Instrument of Music and the Liturgy of the Word

The procession next moves to lectern and pulpit. These are dedicated and the books (and hangings and candles) are put in place. The Old Testament lesson is read, the Gradual Psalm is sung or said, and the

Epistle follows. Those provided in the text of the service may be used, or appropriate selections for the day (if a Sunday, Major Feast, or Patronal Festival) may be substituted. Then the instrument of music is dedicated and used before the Gospel for instrumental music or to accompany a hymn or anthem. The Gospel follows. A sermon may be preached, or a representative of the parish may "outline the plans of the congregation for witness to the Gospel" and "the bishop may respond, indicating the place of this congregation within the life of the diocese." If the Apostles' Creed has not been used when the font was consecrated, the Nicene Creed follows.

Other Offices

A Pastoral Office may follow. Perhaps the most appropriate would be the blessing of oil for the sick (with the laying on of hands and anointing).

The Prayers of the People

The Prayers of the People are led by the deacon or a member of the congregation. It would be appropriate to draft a special form for this occasion or to adapt one of the standard forms. Benefactors and those involved in the building of the church should be commemorated. Concluding prayers are provided. It should be noted that the Litany of Thanksgiving printed after the Additional Directions is not intended for use at the Consecration of a Church, but on occasions after the church has been in use (such as anniversaries of the consecration).

The Consecration of the Altar

The bishop now goes to the altar table and proceeds with the dedication, arms extended. During the last paragraph the bishop lays a hand on the altar and may sign it once (or five times, if crosses are incised in the corners and the center). The altar is sometimes anointed with chrism, but this usage is alien to our rite. When the prayer is finished, the altar is vested and prepared for communion. Flowers may be placed near (but not on) it. Bells may be rung. A eucharistic hymn might be sung while this is taking place. The Peace follows.

The Celebration of the Holy Communion

The service continues with the Offertory. The deed, blueprints, keys, and similar items may be brought forward at the Offertory. The preface of dedication or that of the season or one appropriate to the name of the church may be used. The celebration continues and concludes as usual, the bishop giving the blessing and a deacon or a presbyter the dismissal.

Variants

Portions of the service may be adapted for multipurpose places of worship, multidenominational churches, and private oratories, or for furnishing or parts of a church or chapel. A special order is provided for use in dedicating a church or chapel long in use. For this purpose, a litany of thanksgiving is provided which may also be used on the anniversary of consecration.

Dedication of Church Furnishings and Ornaments
(The Book of Occasional Services)

Some of the material in this section is adapted from the rite in *The Book of Common Prayer* for the Dedication and Consecration of a Church. The dedications are to be used (unless otherwise noted) after the sermon (and Creed) at the Eucharist or at the time of the anthem after the collects at the Daily Office. Two dedications (an altar and a font) are reserved to a bishop by the rubrics of *The Book of Common Prayer*; custom suggests that dedications of chalices and patens and a bell also be reserved to a bishop. As the rubrics of the service note:

In accordance with a venerable tradition, church furnishings and ornaments are consecrated by being put to the use for which they were intended.

The implication is clearly that the forms provided for dedication are desirable but not essential.

The dedications of an altar and a font are taken directly from *The Book of Common Prayer.* The altar is dedicated immediately before the Peace. The form is that of *The Book of Common Prayer,* with the addition of an antiphon, versicle, and response at the beginning. The font is properly dedicated at a baptism—in which case its dedication will immediately precede the Thanksgiving over the Water. Otherwise, it comes in the customary place for dedications. The forms are those in the Prayer Book, with this exception: an antiphon precedes the versicle and response and the prayer follows rather than precedes the versicle and response. Water may be blessed with the form from the Dedication and Consecration of a Church if there are no baptisms.

For all other items to be dedicated, the following material is provided:

> antiphon, versicle, and response:
> prayer of dedication.

We note that, unlike the Prayer Book form, this has no sentence of dedication, which is redundant when preceded by a prayer that serves the same purpose. According to the Jewish roots of Christian liturgy, something is blessed or dedicated by thanking God over it and acknowledging the purpose for which God intended it. The ancient ritual gesture would be to extend the hand toward the item or to lay a hand upon it. In more recent times, the sign of the cross has come to be the most common gesture; and because the sign is connected with the word "bless" or the trinitarian formula, people have come to expect the word "bless" or its equivalent in the prayer, or a sentence of dedication with the trinitarian formula. This explains the redundant sentence in *The Book of Common Prayer* and Dennis Michno's insertion of words in the prayers of dedication. Both are unnecessary. Objects may be censed when dedicated, if incense is customary in the parish. In the Roman Rite objects are aspersed with holy water when blessed, but while this has become common Anglo-Catholic practice, it has no real roots in Anglican liturgical tradition.

The antiphons may be said or sung by all, by the officiant, or by another person. If the forms are sung, the antiphons will be sung to an antiphon tone, the versicle and response to the suffrages tone, and the collect to a collect tone.

The longer form of dedication consists of the following:

1. Presentation of the gift to the celebrant;

2. Sets of versicles and responses;

3. A general prayer of dedication;

4. The proper form of dedication;

5. A collect, if desired, commemorating benefactors or those memorialized by the gift.

All of this material, except for the presentation, might also be sung to appropriate tones.

Restoration of Things Profaned
(The Book of Occasional Services)

With the present increase in church vandalism, this rite will find more use than might once have been expected. The sense of violation which acts of vandalism evoke from a congregation makes this rite pastorally very useful. While the rubrics suggest the bishop as the celebrant, the presbyter in charge of the parish is likely in most cases to be the celebrant.

The rite consists of the following:

1. a procession, for which Psalm 118 with an antiphon is suggested;

2. a declaration of restoration, during which the celebrant may touch the object profaned or extend a hand toward it (incense or water may also be used as symbols of cleansing);

3. a prayer said by the celebrant in the midst of the church.

The procession and the use of water and incense are optional. While use of water in blessings is not native to Anglican tradition, its use here for cleansing is entirely appropriate. It is fitting to use this brief rite immediately before the first service after the profanation has occurred. It may also be pastorally desirable to use the prayer or some portion of the rite at other services on that day.

Secularizing a Consecrated Building
(**The Book of Occasional Services**)

A bishop presides at this service, or appoints a minister as deputy to preside. The altar(s) and all consecrated and dedicated furnishings to be preserved are removed before the service. The order includes:

1. an address by the Presiding Minister;

2. the reading of the Letter of Secularization;

3. appropriate prayers, a blessing, and (if desired) the Peace.

The rite properly acknowledges the sense of loss that such an occasion evokes.

An Afterword: An Appropriate Style

Ceremonial guides more often than not seem to presuppose that there is *one right way* to conduct worship. The generally uniform text of services in prior editions of *The Book of Common Prayer* has fostered this presupposition, even though the rubrics printed with these texts were open to a variety of interpretations. The result seems to have been a number of guides which set out very different "correct" interpretations of the rubrics.

The presupposition of this book is that there is no one right way to conduct worship. The style of worship should, rather, be appropriate to the context. Appropriate is a word which occurs again and again both in the rubrics of the Prayer Book and in the text of this book. It is time to turn our attention now to some of the factors which need to be taken into account in determining what liturgical style is appropriate in a given situation. The following are among the more important factors:

1. the Anglican theological tradition;

2. the social and cultural context;

3. the particular traditions of a parish;

4. the personal convictions of the celebrant;

5. the building in which the worship is conducted;

6. the size and character of the congregation gathered for a particular service;

7. the nature of the occasion for which the congregation has gathered.

We turn now to explore these factors in more detail.

1. The Anglican theological tradition

The "body language" of our ceremonial style is one of the ways that we communicate the Gospel. Our ceremonial style and our worship as a whole need to be consistent with the Gospel we proclaim. Worship, for example, which proclaims the priesthood of all believers but gives all the "action" in worship to the ordained sends out very mixed signals. Worship which proclaims the radical inclusiveness of Jesus Christ but by its language, intentionally or unintentionally, leaves groups feeling excluded, is a scandalous contradiction. Worship which seeks to embody the hospitality of God but discourages congregational warmth does not make sense. Worship which gives absolute allegiance to any political authority is idolatrous.

Worship needs to be theologically consistent with the Gospel, in other words. As Anglican worship, it also needs to conform to the way Episcopalians understand and interpret the Gospel—to the Anglican theological tradition. On the whole, that is an inclusive tradition and allows for a diversity of interpretations, but we still need to respect its integrity. Roman Catholic rubrics superimposed on an Anglican rite simply produce liturgical incoherence. We are under no compulsion to avoid a certain ceremonial practice simply because Roman Catholics (or Lutherans or Presbyterians) employ it, but we need to be sure that it is consistent with the theology of the liturgical texts which we use in worship and with our own theological tradition.

2. The Social and Cultural Context

The ceremonial of our worship needs to be appropriate to the social and cultural context of the congregation. What we should aim for is a distinctly, though not narrowly or restrictively, American expression of the Christian Gospel in our worship. Despite our English roots, a fascination with all things British today does not improve our worship, but hampers it. While the precedents of English law and custom in worship as in other affairs may be instructive, they are not binding for us. Christ becomes incarnate in every culture: he does not wear foreign trappings in our midst, though he retains the capacity to transcend all social and cultural distinctions.

The pluralistic character of American culture, and the multiple ethnic roots of the American people, mean that there will be a diversity of liturgical style, depending on the make-up of any given congregation.

3. The Particular Traditions of a Parish

Episcopal parishes manifest a considerable diversity in their theological, liturgical, and ethnic traditions. Every tradition must be tested against evangelical truth and catholic tradition, but on the whole this diversity is commendable. Celebrants should respect the liturgical style of the parishes in which they conduct worship. To fail to take into account a parish's preference for evangelical simplicity or for catholic ceremonial or to ignore the ethnic roots and traditions of a significant number of parishioners is to fail to relate to people as they really are. Presbyters may seek to move their parish from the periphery of Anglican liturgical or theological tradition toward the center or to broaden a narrow cultural or ethnic base, but they need to be sensitive to the traditions of the parish as they do so. Worship also needs to be adapted to the resources of a parish.

Parishes should make full uses of the talents and gifts of their parishioners in their worship, but at the same time they should not try to go beyond what they are capable of in trying to emulate the way worship is conducted elsewhere. A besetting temptation of parish choirs, for example, has been to attempt—usually unsuccessfully, and inappropriately as well—to adopt music intended for a cathedral setting.

4. The Personal Convictions of the Celebrant

If clergy need to respect the integrity of a parish's tradition, so parishes need to respect the theological and liturgical integrity of one who presides at their worship. Celebrants should conform to the style of the parish insofar as possible, but should not be asked to do violence to their conscience in the process. Clergy and parishes both need to learn to adapt to each other in this matter. No one leading a parish's worship should be asked to adopt a ceremonial style which is uncomfortable. When this happens, it has an impact on the integrity and credibility of the service. In addition, assistants at the altar need to conform to the style of the celebrant. To have concelebrants at the altar who use different ceremonial gestures is distracting to the congregation and undermines the coherence of the service.

5. The Building in which the worship is conducted

Ceremonial needs to be adapted to the size, the acoustics, and the layout of the building where it takes place. Large gestures look ridiculous in a small space; intimate gestures may become insignificant in a vast space. Celebrants (and others with specific functions in a service) need to adapt their voice to the acoustics of the space, so that they may be heard, yet not overwhelm with their voices. Processions, ways of administering communion and baptism, and other liturgical actions must all be adapted to the layout of a building. Our buildings need to be adapted for worship according to our present Prayer Book, but services also need to be adapted to the possibilities and limitations of the building.

6. The size and character of the congregation

An intimate and less formal style suits a small group gathered for worship; careful planning is important for liturgical action with large gatherings of people. A sensitive celebrant will preside over worship for different groups of people in different ways. The approaches to a mixed congregation, a predominantly older congregation, and a predominantly younger congregation will be different. The celebrant needs to take into account the make-up of the congregation gathered for worship and to adjust accordingly.

7. The nature of the occasion

An Easter service has a different tone and shape from a Lenten service or an Advent service or a Christmas Service. In the same way, an ordinary weekday Eucharist should be in a lower key than a Sunday or feast day Eucharist. The Eucharist for a wedding has a different tone from that for a burial. A "sameness" of style is inappropriate to different occasions. In the past, services could only be adapted to various occasions, festive or penitential, by adding onto them and making them longer. This is no longer the case. The 1979 *Book of Common Prayer* makes far more provision for adjusting the way in which the Eucharist is celebrated on various occasions than prior editions have done. In planning services, full use should be made of such provisions.

Planning Appropriate Worship

Appropriate worship does not just happen. It is the result of careful planning. Ideally, more than just the celebrant will be involved in such planning. The professional staff of a parish should work together, and worship committees—ongoing or *ad hoc* for a season or a particular service—are useful as well. In planning pastoral offices, such as weddings and funerals, the persons involved should take part in the planning, working within guidelines established by a parish.

A service at its best is an integrated whole—lessons, prayers, hymns, anthems, sermon, and ceremonial actions fit together. Only coordinated planning can make this happen. The greater flexibility of the present edition of the Prayer Book also calls for more careful planning. Celebrants sometimes resist planning and rehearsing services in the conviction that this undermines "spontaneity." Spontaneity at its best, however, does not mean doing whatever comes into one's head in the midst of worship. It means adjusting and adapting as appropriate in the course of worship. Lack of planning does not create the impression of spontaneity: at its worst, it gives the impression that someone has not thought ahead about what is going to happen and is making it up as things go along! Authentic spontaneity in liturgical worship finds its place within an ordered whole which incorporates both the lives of the gathered community and the liturgical tradition of the Church.

Graceful worship is carefully planned and thought-out, open to the movement of God's spirit but careful to include the best talents of all those involved. Careful planning enables us to "worship the Lord in the beauty of holiness," to worship the Lord "decently and in order," to worship the Lord "in spirit and in truth."

A Short List of Resources

The lists that follow are not intended to be exhaustive. They include the books and other resources that the author has found to be most helpful in liturgical planning and in addressing the issues dealt with in this book.

Official Liturgical and Musical Texts

The following books are published by The Church Hymnal Corporation in cooperation with the Standing Liturgical Commission and the Standing Commission on Church Music.

The Book of Common Prayer (1979)

Lesser Feasts and Fasts

The Book of Occasional Services

The Altar Book

Ministry to the Sick

Lectionary Texts (in 5 volumes: Years A, B, and C; Lesser Feasts and Fasts; and Various Occasions and Occasional Services)

The Book of Gospels

Daily Office Readings (Year 1, volumes 1, 2; Year 2, volumes 1, 2)

Daily Office Book (incorporates the Daily Office materials from the Prayer Book and *Daily Office Readings*)

The Hymnal 1982

Gradual Psalms (in 5 volumes: Years A, B, and C; Holy Days and Various Occasions; Lesser Feasts and Fasts)

The Anglican Chant Psalter

Other Liturgical and Musical Texts

The books and resources in this list are not official publications of the Episcopal Church. They include recent significant prayer books of other churches, an enriched version of the office material in our Book of Common Prayer, and musical resources for our own texts.

The Book of Alternative Services of the Anglican Church of Canada, Toronto, Anglican Book Center, 1985.

> Our Canadian sister has produced a book of Rite II services closely akin to our own. This is a work of considerable merit. It shows greater sensitivity to inclusive language than our own book. Reference is made above to the psalter collects of this book.

The Lutheran Book of Worship (also available in the Minister's Desk Edition and the Accompaniment Edition, each of which has supplementary materials), Minneapolis, Augsburg Publishing House, 1975.

> Coming from a similar liturgical tradition, *The Lutheran Book of Worship* has materials which merit our attention. Reference is made above to the psalm tones and psalter collects of this book.

Book of Worship, United Church of Christ, New York, Office for Church Life and Leadership, 1986.

> This book, which comes out of a church with roots in the Congregational and Evangelical and Reformed traditions, is remarkably similar to our own Book of Common Prayer. Its attention to inclusive language is noteworthy, and its consistent use of inclusive language is almost always graceful.

Howard Galley, editor, *The Prayer Book Office*, New York, Seabury, 1980.

> This book contains the Daily Office, Rite II, from the Book of Common Prayer, with antiphons for psalms and canticles, a selection of readings from Christian literature, and similar materials, along with ceremonial notes. A new edition of this book should soon be in print.

Gordon Lathrop and Gail Ramshaw-Schmidt, editors, *Lectionary for the Christian People, Cycle A of the Roman, Episcopal, and Lutheran Lectionaries, Revised Standard Version texts emended*. New York, Pueblo, 1986.

> This lectionary, edited for inclusive language, is not yet authorized for use in the Episcopal Church, but deserves our attention as perhaps the most graceful and acceptable of the inclusive language translations.

James Barrett, *The Psalmnary*, 1982, available from Hymnary Press, 1317 Sorenson Drive, Helena, Montana 59601.

> Many will find the pointing of the psalms (to Sarum tones) in this work easier to read than in *Gradual Psalms*. The refrains have been composed by the editor.

Peter Hallock, *The Ionian Psalter*, available from Ionian Arts, Inc., P.O. Box 259, Mercer Island WA 98040-0259, 1986 ff.

> These are settings of the gradual psalms in harmonized chant (through-composed for easier singing) with congregational refrains. This collection is in process of publication. Psalms for Year A, Advent through Trinity Sunday, are now available.

Available from Mason Martens, 175 West 72 Street, New York, NY 10023: *The Eucharistic Prayers of Rite II* (settings of the prayers to the Ambrosian preface tone and a tone based on the Te Deum melody); *Simple Kyriale* (plainsong settings of the Rite II texts of the Ordinary of the Eucharist); *Fraction Anthems* (settings of all texts in *The Book of Occasional Services* and seven additional texts); *Music for Holy Week; Passions for Holy Week.*

> Mason Martens is a talented musical editor and a leading scholar of plainsong. His editions are a valuable musical resource to the church.

Ceremonial Rules and Rationale

While there are any number of books available in this field, those listed below have been particularly significant to the author in formulating guidelines for ceremonial practice.

Marion J. Hatchett, *A Manual of Ceremonial for the New Prayer Book,* Sewanee, St. Luke's Journal of Theology, 1977.

> The first and still the best brief ceremonial guide to *The Book of Common Prayer* 1979.

Manual on the Liturgy, Lutheran Book of Worship, Minneapolis, Augsburg, 1979.

> The official ceremonial guide to *The Lutheran Book of Worship.*

Aidan Kavanagh, OSB, *Elements of Rite,* New York, Pueblo, 1982.

> With considerable wit and insight, Fr. Kavanagh presents in apodictic form rules for good liturgy that are worth taking very seriously.

Cheslyn Jones, Geoffrey Wainwright, and Edward Yarnold, SJ, editors, *The Study of Liturgy,* New York, Oxford, 1978.

> A collection of essays which cover the theology and history of worship, the regular services of the church, ordination, the calendar, and the setting of worship (ceremonial, music, architecture, and vestments), as well as pastoral aspects of worship.

The Theology of Worship

Our worship and ceremonial should be grounded in a theological understanding of what we are engaged in. The books listed below represent only a sampling of a large number of important books available in this field. The first five books are from other traditions. The last two are significant commentaries on *The Book of Common Prayer* 1979.

J.J. von Allmen, *Worship: Its Theology and Practice,* New York, Oxford, 1965.

> This is a profound work by a liturgist in the Reformed tradition, which considers the issues related to the Sunday Eucharist as the normative worship of the Church.

Alexander, Schmemann, *Introduction to Liturgical Theology,* London, Faith Press, 1966.

_____ , *For the Life of the World* (also published at times under the titles *Sacraments and Orthodoxy* and *The World as Sacrament*), Crestwood, New York, St. Vladimir's Press, 1973.

> These two books present an important theological study of sacramental worship from an Orthodox perspective.

Louis Bouyer, *Liturgical Piety* (also published under the title *Life and Liturgy*), South Bend, Indiana, Notre Dame, 1955.

> A seminal work in liturgical theology by a Roman Catholic scholar.

Tad Guzie, *The Book of Sacramental Basics,* New York/Ramsey, New Jersey, Paulist Press, 1981.

> A provocative rethinking of sacramental theology by a Roman Catholic scholar.

Marion J. Hatchett, *Commentary on the American Prayer Book,* New York, Seabury, 1980.

> This is the standard commentary on *The Book of Common Prayer* 1979.

Leonel L. Mitchell, *Praying Shapes Believing,* Minneapolis, Winston, 1985.

> This is a thoughtful theological study by one of the church's leading liturgical scholars.

Resources for Planning Services

Marion J. Hatchett, *A Manual for Clergy and Church Musicians,* New York, Church Hymnal Corporation, 1980.

> This is an extraordinarily useful book on how to plan music for services. The Check Lists for Planning Services in the Appendix are very helpful; a parish, once it has settled into the range of options it will use, can make up its own check lists based on these. It is to be hoped that a new edition of this book will be issued to bring it into conformity with *The Hymnal* 1982.

Marion J. Hatchett, *Hymnal Studies Five: A Liturgical Index to the Hymnal 1982,* New York, Church Hymnal Corporation, 1986.

> This useful book suggests hymns for every service in the authorized liturgical texts of this church. Suggestions are based on the lectionary and appropriate themes for each service. The suggestions should be used with discretion, and in accordance with the recommendations of the author in the Introduction. The book draws on the whole Hymnal, and its suggestions need to be adapted to the hymn repertoire of a particular congregation.

The Episcopal Church Lesson Calendar, Wilton, Connecticut, Morehouse-Barlow Company, issued annually.

> This calendar provides also a listing of propers for the Office and the Eucharist each day, with a suggested entrance hymn and "hymn of the day" for Sundays and Principal Feasts. There are useful seasonal hymn lists, as well as a list of suggested collects at the Prayers of the People. Other useful ceremonial notes and suggestions (proper blessings, hymns in place of the Phos hilaron, canticles at the Eucharist and the Office, and so on) are also provided. Howard E. Galley, Jr., and Robert D. Gillespie are the current editors of this, which the author considers the single best guide to service planning.

Index

Aaronic blessing, 176
Ablutions, 124, 139, 140, 182, 189
Absolution, 35, 52, 60, 67, 73, 75, 76,
   84, 95, 142, 161, 163, 166
Academic insignia, 33
   gown, 11–12
   hood, 11, 12
   tippet, 11, 12, 15
Acclamations, 59, 61, 62, 63–64, 65,
   66, 112, 148, 180, 186
   at the Eucharist, 172
   Good Friday, 92
   memorial, 124, 125, 132
   Rite II memorial, 132, 135
Acolytes, 47, 58, 70, 93, 96, 124, 126,
   196, 200
Acts of the Apostles, 68
Addresses, 97, 98, 150, 160, 187, 196,
   198
   introductory, 172, 200
Adoration of the Crucified, 91, 92,
   93–94
Advent, 3, 12, 43, 46, 53, 54, 64, 65,
   66, 73, 75, 80, 105
   service of lessons and carols, 46
   festival of lessons and music, 106
Advertisements (Archbishop Parker's),
   10, 14
Affirmation, bishop's, 191
Affusion, 115, 117–18
Agape, 90
Agnus Dei, 27, 126, 137
Alb, 8–9, 10, 11, 14, 15
All Hallows' Eve
   Service for, 46
   Vigil for, 106–07
All Saints, Feast of, 43
All Saints' Day or Sunday, 3, 4, 109, 110
   Vigil Eucharist of, 46, 50, 79, 101,
   102

Alleluia, 36, 50, 82, 101
   double, 141
   Easter, 100, 137
   Verse or Tract, 58, 68, 187
Altar, 199, 206
   consecration of, 202–03
   dedication of, 202, 204
   free-standing, 13–, 137
   "of repose," 88
   stripping the, 90
   table, 16, 17–18, 25, 123, 202
   team, 6
Altar Book, The, 28, 40, 45, 49, 50, 58,
   65, 68, 73, 74, 85, 92, 93, 95, 97,
   98, 116, 127, 132, 135, 138, 141,
   150, 157, 160, 190
Ambrosian Rite, 44
Amen, the, 125, 135, 141, 174
American Episcopal Church, 13
Amice, 9
Anglican Chant, 68, 98, 160, 171
Anglican Chant Psalter, The, 33, 38, 84
Anglican Church of Canada, 91, 142
Anglican Communion, 91
Anglican Eucharistic theology, 88
Anglican introit, 53
Anglican liturgical tradition, 205
Anglican Office, 40
Anglican rite, 186, 208
Anglican theological tradition, 90, 207,
   208
Anglican tradition, 47, 74, 131, 183,
   206
Anglo-Catholic practice, 205
Announcements, 126
Annunciation, Feast of the, 43
Anointing, 163, 164–65, 167–68, 202
Anthems, 26, 27, 28, 44, 61, 63, 66, 75,
   86, 89, 93, 94, 95, 103, 106, 125,
   128, 137, 152, 154, 155, 156, 159,